NF
346.7304
SUMM

W9-CER-531

3-24-11

The COMPLETE LANDLORD & PROPERTY MANAGER'S *Legal Survival Kit*

Trimble Co. Public Library
P.O. Box 249
Bedford,, KY 40006

DIANA BRODMAN SUMMERS
ATTORNEY AT LAW

sphinx
publishing

Copyright © 2010 by Diana Brodman Summers
Cover and internal design © 2010 by Sourcebooks, Inc.

All rights reserved. No part of this book may be reproduced in any form or by any electronic or mechanical means including information storage and retrieval systems—except in the case of brief quotations embodied in critical articles or reviews—without permission in writing from its publisher, Sourcebooks, Inc. Sourcebooks and the colophon are registered trademarks of Sourcebooks, Inc. All brand names and product names used in this book are trademarks, registered trademarks, or trade names of their respective holders. Sourcebooks, Inc., is not associated with any product or vendor in this book.

First Edition: 2010

Published by: **Sphinx® Publishing, An Imprint of Sourcebooks, Inc.®**
Naperville Office
P.O. Box 4410, Naperville, Illinois 60567-4410
(630) 961-3900
Fax: (630) 961-2168
www.sourcebooks.com
www.SphinxLegal.com

This publication is designed to provide accurate and authoritative information in regard to the subject matter covered. It is sold with the understanding that the publisher is not engaged in rendering legal, accounting, or other professional service. If legal advice or other expert assistance is required, the services of a competent professional person should be sought.

From a Declaration of Principles Jointly Adopted by a Committee of the American Bar Association and a Committee of Publishers and Associations

This product is not a substitute for legal advice.
Disclaimer required by Texas statutes.

Library of Congress Cataloging-in-Publication Data.

Summers, Diana Brodman.
  The complete landlord and property manager's legal survival kit / Diana Brodman Summers.
    p. cm.
  1. Landlord and tenant—United States—Popular works. 2. Leases—United States—Popular works. 3. Rent—United States—Popular works. I. Title.
  KF590.Z9S86 2010
  346.7304'34—dc22

                                    2009036602

Printed and bound in the United States of America.
VP 10 9 8 7 6 5 4 3 2 1

Contents

SECTION 2: STYLES OF LANDLORDS AND GETTING HELP

SECTION 3: LAWS THAT IMPACT LANDLORDS

SECTION 4: THE LEASE

SECTION 5: THE RENTAL AMOUNT

SECTION 6: PREPARING THE PROPERTY

**SECTION 8: TENANTS—PART 2
THE BAD AND THE UGLY**

SECTION 9: SECURITY DEPOSITS

Introduction

As author of *Landlord's Legal Guide in Illinois*, *How to Buy Your First Home,* and *The Home Buyer's Answer Book,* I had the opportunity to meet with many people who were facing the daunting prospect of becoming landlords, either by design or because they were unable to sell their property. They all had two things in common: concerns about how to be a good landlord, and questions about where to turn for help. This book should help with both of these concerns.

The purpose of this book is to prepare the landlord for the landlord/tenant relationship. My goal has been to create an all-around reference book that will at least provide some direction to both the seasoned landlord and the brand-new landlord. While the area of landlord/tenant laws and procedures is huge, this little book sifts out the important issues and presents them in an easy-to-read format. Links to landlord/tenant laws are included as are links to a host of websites that will assist both new and experienced landlords.

HOW TO USE THIS BOOK

This book is divided up into sections with multiple chapters in each section. A section is an individual issue that has multiple topics which explain the issue. The chapters discuss topics that need further clarification. My suggestion is that you read through the entire book once—yes, even those chapters that you think you know—and then use the book as a reference tool for solving future problems.

Let's look at the contents of the book:

Section 1 contains an overview of the past financial history of real estate, how the major problems in the economy have been influenced by the real estate industry, how legislators have stepped in to correct these problems, how this all affects landlords, and what landlords can expect in the future.

Section 2 looks at the general types of landlords and the primary help available for each type. We begin with a self-test to find out what type of landlord you are. As for getting help, in the next chapters we discuss property managers, attorneys, tradespeople, and how the landlord can deal with each of these groups like an expert.

In Section 3 we look at the laws that impact renting. We explore the federal laws on discrimination, EPA hazards, and other protection issues. We look at the impact of state and local laws, and help the landlord find these laws in his or her own location. Finally we discuss what landlords need to do if they are accused of a legal violation, with an emphasis on the most common violation—housing discrimination.

Section 4 is all about the lease. We talk about where you can get a lease, how you can write your own lease, and what clauses are important for a lease. In addition to creating a lease, we provide information on changing the lease and on the ceremony of signing the lease.

Section 5 is about everyone's favorite subject, getting money or being paid rent. We look at the rental payment from how to determine how much to charge, to the actual collection of rent, to a variety of rent modifications that a landlord may run into.

In Section 6 we prepare the property for the tenant. This includes coming to grips with renting out your family home and what you should do to protect your family's belongings. We discuss renting out a vacation home and what you can do to make your property a great place for vacationers. Then we discuss insurance and the changes needed when property is rented. Finally we talk about marketing your rental.

Sections 7 and 8 are all about the tenants. Section 7 is about the good tenants, how to screen people to get good tenants, the benefits of renting to tenants with companion animals, and keeping a good relationship with tenants. Section 8 is about the problem tenants. We start with the extra people who do not pay rent, then we move on to subleasing and other common tenant problems. We end with ways to deal with tenants who want out, tenants you want out, and evictions.

Section 9 is devoted to one of the most misunderstood issues in renting, the security deposit. We cover the basics of security deposits, how to calculate what the tenant gets back, the legal explanation of this fund, and what to do when the property is sold.

In Section 10 we cover the landlord's duty of safety, duty of maintenance, and right of entry.

Finally, in Section 11 we address the concerns of tenants, which does not mean that the landlord cannot read this material. In fact, I urge you to look this over to see what information is important to the tenant.

All the above Sections have references to forms in Appendix C, websites of general interest in Appendix B, and websites for each state in Appendix A.

When reading this book please keep a couple of important things in mind:

- ✪ Laws that control the landlord/tenant relationship differ by location. States, cities, towns, counties, and areas can enact their own laws that dictate requirements and/or procedures. You must follow these laws in addition to the federal laws.

- ✪ What is considered to be standard operating procedure or common practice regarding rentals and/or evictions also differs by location. In many areas, the custom changes by the particular city, county, and court. The people who are the most knowledgeable about your local rental customs and legal requirements are the local realtors and the local attorneys who concentrate in landlord/tenant law.

✪   You can research local laws and practices, but ultimately you will need to rely on local professionals to explain the local laws and practices.

✪   It is impossible for one book to contain all the variations of laws that affect the landlord/tenant relationship in the United States.

*   *   *   *   *

Disclaimer: Nothing in this book implies or should be construed as creating an attorney/client relationship between the reader and the author, Sourcebooks, or any agent thereof.

SECTION 1

UNDERSTANDING THE ECONOMICS

This first Section begins with a look at the housing industry as a whole and how it got where it is today. We show how the once slow-moving industry that lay dormant for decades is now at the center of a major economic slowdown worthy of massive media attention. Next we touch on the latest financial issues of the housing industry that are pertinent to the landlord and the current tools available to fix the problems. We discuss what landlords need to know in order to understand the financial direction of the real estate/housing industry, which is in the middle of major changes. Finally we look to how future changes in the real estate/housing industry will impact how landlords will be doing business from now on.

How Did We Get Here?

This chapter reviews the dramatic changes in the housing market and the economy in the past few years. It discusses how these financial issues have resulted in changes to the real estate/housing industry, applying the changes to landlords with emphasis on situations that today's landlords may find themselves in.

HISTORY OF THE HOUSING MARKET

To understand the housing market today you need to have some basic knowledge of how this market has evolved and the principles of the market that still apply today. The housing market became a force in the U.S. economy after World War II was over and service members returned from the war looking for a place to live. In addition to the returning veterans there was a significant increase in immigration. These immigrants came to the United States looking for a better life. A major part of that better life was buying property, a dream home plus a little extra for when times got tough. Many of the baby boomers can attest to grandparents who worked hard to own a two-flat, three-flat, or apartment building. My grandparents used to say that if they both lost their jobs, at least they would have income from the rent payments. The housing boom was on and those who had property to sell were king. This was a huge sellers' market. The seller determined the price, the amount of down payment, and other terms of the agreement.

This sellers' market continued well into the 1950s. Depending on the region, the housing industry maintained the cycle of sellers' markets when there were more buyers than houses for sale and buyers' markets when there were more houses for sale than buyers. It was a perfect symmetry, and by the 1960s an investment in real estate was considered boringly stable and not a risky place to put money in order to get a minor return. Actually, in the 1960s and into the 1970s a person could get more return on money put into a savings account than money put into property. These investments mirrored the way the U.S. citizens lived—buy a house close to your family, raise your family in that house, and stay there until that house is passed on to your children. It was not unusual for a family to remain in the same house long after its twenty-five-year mortgage was paid off.

By the 1970s enterprising baby boomers started to look at housing as more than just as a place to live or as the two-flat owned by their grandparents, they looked at housing as a potential moneymaker. Rehab was the word. The goal was to find a house that needed work and where the sellers were anxious to get rid of the house (like in a divorce), then buy the house cheap, rehab it, and sell high. By the late 1970s and early 1980s this was a very lucrative cottage industry.

In the late 1980s the real estate market began one of its largest swings upward. The result was higher property prices, quick sales, and lots of available money for real estate financing. In short, we had a very hot sellers' market. The real estate seller was able to set his or her own price, and prices soared.

Lenders looked at this activity and wanted to get in on the profits. The standard requirements to get financing changed. No longer was the buyer required to put up 20% or 25% as a down payment, to have an excellent credit rating, or even to prove that his or her income could handle the mortgage payments. Mortgage money was available for anyone who was willing to sign on the dotted line, as long as the property appraised for more than the amount of the money borrowed. The financial institution made sure all property did appraise high, either

by an accurate appraisal or fudging the numbers, because they, like everyone else, believed that the price of property would never drop. Creative financing like zero-down mortgages and adjustable rate mortgages (with sky-high adjustments) became the norm. Articles were written about the death of the conventional mortgage and the public bought into that idea.

This led to a frenzy of activity for lenders, many of whom loaned money via what are now called sub-prime loans. These loans were for the buyer who could not qualify for a conventional mortgage, for property that did not appraise high enough, and for those who needed to get money out of their property fast. Some lenders took advantage of property owners by selling them a mortgage that the property owner was unable to make payments on, especially mortgages where the interest rate terms could cause the payment amount to double or triple as time went on. The goal of these unscrupulous lenders was to quickly foreclose on the property and then sell the property for a sizable profit. These lenders bet that the real estate market would continue to rise and that the overheated real estate bubble would never burst.

This all worked until the real estate market proved once again that it is cyclical and that all bubbles eventually burst. However, this time the cycle went into a major correction, and it took the economy with it. The correction took many people by surprise. Legitimate mortgage lenders and property owners saw the value of their real estate plummet within a few short weeks. Sales stalled and in some areas stopped completely. Many properties were foreclosed by the lenders, who then were unable to sell the property, and the properties sat vacant. Some cities looked like ghost towns due to all the vacant foreclosed homes.

When the real estate bubble did burst it sent negative waves far beyond the buyers and sellers of property. Financial institutions and speculators who were heavily invested in sub-prime loans were rocked, and we have now found out that almost every financial institution had some amount of capital invested in these loans. As with every real estate buyers' market, the money that was once abundantly available for mortgage lending all but dried up. As a precaution against this ever happening again the mortgage underwriters pulled out the old-fashioned criteria that required borrowers to have a certain credit rating, a large down payment, and sufficient income to be able to pay the monthly mortgage payments—those principles that were touted as being dead less than two years before.

THE ECONOMY

During the past decades experts who watched the real estate industry have issued several statements that we all thought would remain true until the end of time.

- ✪ The housing industry is cyclical. It swings from being a buyers' market to a sellers' market.

- ✪ These cyclical patterns are never extreme changes, but merely minor adjustments of supply and demand.

- ✪ The amount of time that the housing industry is in a buyers' market will be followed by that same length of time as a sellers' market.

- ✪ Real estate will always appreciate in value. An investor can never lose money by buying real estate.

In hindsight, we now know that even though the housing industry remains cyclical and swings from a buyers' market to a sellers' market, those reactions can result in fast and extreme changes. We have seen, in the most recent economy, that there is no accurate indicator of how long the market will favor either buyers or sellers. Unfortunately we also now know that real estate can significantly drop in value.

The economy took a huge hit when the real estate industry went into correction for a number of reasons. Three primary reasons were: 1) so many people and institutions had invested in the sub-prime loans that a loss in sub-prime funds affected everyone, including those who only had what were thought to be solid 401(k) investments; 2) too many people, regardless of ability, wanted to get into the get-rich-quick scheme in real estate, so the losses spread beyond the real estate industry, builders, and bankers, and into the middle class; and 3) huge increases in the sales price of real estate far outpaced any increases in salaries or increases in the number of jobs available. This constant rise in the price of housing caused those who wanted a home to financially extend themselves way beyond what they were able to pay back from their existing salaries.

The idea of living on credit cards and having a huge debt became the norm. This change in the attitude about credit spread through the United States and even into how the country dealt with borrowing from other countries. This all came to a head in late 2008 when the number of foreclosures and the number of job losses hit an all-time high. At that point, the unthinkable happened—property values began to plunge. Lenders who agreed to inflated appraisals in order to make huge loans were now caught up in foreclosures where the real value of the property was sometimes half or less than half of the money owed.

For many people, it was these changes in our economy that have brought them into the ranks of landlords.

Fixing Problems

This chapter discusses the financial problems that may have caused you to become a landlord, or maybe are just about to make you give up being a landlord—along with some answers. If you are an experienced landlord who has been renting out property for over a decade many of the industry standards that you have relied upon are changing. If you are new to being a landlord you will find that some of the new attitudes about renting are counter-intuitive to what you have thought or heard.

THE ECONOMY'S EFFECT ON LANDLORDS

You may have arrived at the point of being a landlord because of the changes in the real estate market. Those changes may have allowed you to obtain some of the aforementioned "easy money" to finance your property. Or you may, like many other property owners, have taken on more debt than wise through a sub-prime financing plan.

Traditional Effects

Many in the rental industry tend to forget that they are part of what is loosely referred to as the housing market. The fact is, when the real estate market is on the rise, which favors home sellers and encourages homeownership, the rental market slips, with fewer tenants and lower rents. When the real estate market is falling, the reverse is true. The recent problems in the real estate market have dramatically illustrated this relationship.

On one hand, prior to the recent crash, the availability of money for mortgage loans, refinancing, and home improvement loans increased. This allowed existing landlords to use their property as collateral to purchase more rental property, secure loans on their rental property for remodeling, and refinance high-rate mortgages at lower interest rates. (This includes those landlords who decided to refinance their rental property as a way to take funds out of the property for other uses.) On the other hand, landlords were hit with a major negative. The easy money also allowed more people to purchase their own homes and leave the rentals. That, in turn, caused the pool of qualified renters to significantly drop in many areas, leading to a decrease in the amount that landlords could charge for rent.

When the real estate market is in a major correction, landlords find themselves in the same position as other property owners. The major difference is that landlords are in the business of using their property as a way to generate a monthly income. Now, just like others who borrowed when money was readily available, landlords must adjust their plans to deal with the most recent market correction.

The Investors   In addition to these standard things landlords expected, the most recent housing crisis, with its heavy activity by investors, has had unexpected effects on the rental industry. Many of those who purchased homes or condos as investments or with an eye to a teardown/rebuild have found it impossible to get any money out of their investment. Like non-investors who are attempting to sell their homes, investors have found a lack of buyers for their properties. Investors who purchased property for teardown are not only having problems selling the not-yet-built mansion, they are being thwarted by cities that have recently enacted laws to prevent the rabid teardowns that plagued many older areas during the height of the overheated market.

The number of investors and owners who have decided to rent out their property is so important that it now has a name: "the shadow market." This separates the purchased-for-resale properties from properties purchased to be rentals. For those who keep statistics on rentals, the shadow market is negatively impacting the traditional rental market. Generally, tenants are able to pay lower rents for properties that were intended for sale than for the usual multi-tenant rentals.

UNEXPECTED LANDLORDS

All of the above, in addition to the real estate cyclical boom and subsequent correction, have brought a brand new type of landlord into the mix—the unexpected or unplanned landlord. This is the person who, because of financial issues directly caused by the real estate correction, has been put into the position of renting out his or her property.

You may be reading this book because you have become an accidental or unexpected landlord—one of thousands who purchased a home, rental property, or a vacation home when the market was high and now cannot sell it without taking a loss. You are faced with several options: sell your property for much less than you owe on it; leave the property vacant and keep up the mortgage payments; stop paying the mortgage and face foreclosure; or become a landlord.

The decision to rent out your property rather than take a financial loss is wise and rewarding. The real estate market is cyclical and the current buyers' market will return to a sellers' market in the future. Judging by past performance, your property will, in the long term, increase in value. The issue is just how long the long term is. Right now the most prudent action is to rent out the property for an amount that covers your expenses and upkeep on the property, and that (hopefully) generates a small profit. In the future, when the real estate market again cycles into a sellers' market, you will be able to sell and get your investment out of the property with little or no financial loss.

FINANCIAL PROBLEMS ON RENTAL PROPERTY

Many landlords got caught up borrowing easy money as a way to buy or refinance their rental property. They now face mortgage payments that continue to rise due to the creative financing used. There is no getting around the fact that this is a very serious condition that can easily result in foreclosure. If the lender should foreclose, it takes away any potential the landlord has of using this rental property to help them out of debt.

Once the landlord realizes that mortgage payments are rising faster than rent, the landlord needs to sit down and assess what he or she actually has and what options there are to increase revenue.

Increasing Rents

If you find yourself needing to increase revenue from your rental property, look at the current leases to see if you can increase the rent to match the increased mortgage payment. You may even want to hire an attorney who is experienced in landlord/tenant law to help you in adjusting leases or taking other action that will bring in more money.

For new tenants, of course, you should start their tenancy at the higher rental price and be sure to include a clause in the new lease that allows the rent to be increased under certain circumstances.

Furthermore, with some work unused areas in a rental property (such as a basement) may be able to produce income as a garden apartment or a locked storage area. The landlord may also be able to rent out garage space or parking space on the rental property.

Refinancing and Other Places for Assistance

While you are looking at ways to raise income, you should also work toward refinancing into a conventional mortgage. A conventional mortgage is one in which the payments stay the same, month after month. In a rental situation where you are dealing with long-term leases without the ability to raise the rent, keeping an adjustable rate mortgage, with mortgage payments that can significantly increase, is asking for problems.

In 2009 the federal government began a plan to provide financial assistance for property owners. Before you miss one more mortgage payment or sink into foreclosure you should look into what the government has to offer. The primary website for this assistance is www. makinghomeaffordable.gov. While this 2009 program expires in 2010, it is expected that new programs will take its place. Check for those new plans at www.hud.gov and www.fha.gov. Please take a moment to look at what is available to you from the federal government.

You may also be able to get assistance in obtaining a conventional mortgage from the city your property is located in, or from local lending institutions who want to invest in your area. It is common for local community groups to take an active stand in helping those who own property in the area. Landlords who rent to members of the community are often able to obtain financial assistance in order to continue to provide housing for local residents.

*   *   *   *   *

Being a landlord can be very financially rewarding. Real property always increases in value over a period of time; traditionally, property has been a sound long-term investment. People need a place to live so there will always be a need for rental property, even when the economy is at it lowest. Do not let this temporary correction in the financial and real estate market deter you from enjoying the rewards of the rental business.

The Future of Renting

In this chapter we discuss the future of the rental industry and how to adapt to what is ahead. Landlords will need to have a working knowledge of the industry and its future in order to make successful decisions about their rental property. This knowledge will guide you in even the smallest decisions, such as when do you upgrade your property and when is leaving it alone the best financial decision.

LEARN YOUR INDUSTRY

Property or land will always have an intrinsic value, that is, land will never be worth zero. The pricing of what we call real estate includes both the land and the structure set on top of it—the building. Again, the value of real estate will probably never go down to zero, absent some major calamity. The value of a property is determined by many factors including the cost of rebuilding, the cost of nearby structures, the makeup of the neighborhood, the durability of the structure, etc. Even in neighborhoods where values have significantly dipped, the home prices will eventually increase. The problem is, that increase might not happen in the course of a normal person's life-span.

We have seen that the real estate industry can be volatile and can burn those who are not watching for changes. Recently those who ignored the principles of a high down payment, a conventional mortgage, and keeping housing costs to about 36% of gross income overextended themselves, leading to a rash of foreclosures. The best advice that any current homeowner can get is to reduce debt and bring what is owed on your property in line with what the property is worth—easy to say and tough to do.

For landlords this means keeping your attention on the property: not letting a bad tenant ruin your property or drive good tenants out; not making errors that can lower the value of your property or get you sued; keeping up the maintenance on your property; and making the extra effort to screen tenants and to follow the laws.

As for the economy and the cycles in the real estate industry, watch the indicators. For years, many of my colleagues and I wondered how a normal middle-income person could afford a home in some of our bigger cities. We saw in our own suburbs that our police officers, our teachers, and our fire fighters could not afford to live in the city they worked in because the price of houses had gone up so quickly. It was not unusual to see homes sold for a profit of over $25,000 in as little as a month. For many of us this was not an indicator of a time to invest, but an indicator that a correction was looming and that we needed to shore up our own investments.

If you watch these types of indicators, you too can predict if the real estate industry is going into a buyers' or sellers' market. What you need to do is read information that is readily available in the real estate section of your local newspaper, your closest big city newspaper, and a financial newspaper. Most local newspapers list when a home is sold and what the selling price was; in most states that is public information. By following the real estate ads you will see the amount it was first listed for and compare that to the amount it sold for.

As a property owner this is important. You can determine when it is time to refinance to get a mortgage with lower monthly payments or go from an adjustable rate mortgage to a conventional one. You can decide that you need to continue to rent out your property because holding it will only increase the value and give you a larger sales price. In other words, you can determine how long to wait before putting your home on the market.

As a landlord you can watch what other rentals are going for and then determine when is the right time to raise or lower the rent. You can decide that since few people are renting and more are buying, you need to hold on to your tenants. Or you can see a decrease in money available for mortgages, meaning fewer people will be able to buy and that you will therefore have a larger pool of prospective tenants.

THE ECONOMIC FUTURE FOR THE LANDLORD

One of the primary benefits of the latest economic downturn is that for the housing industry we have gone back to following those old tried and true rules. This should stabilize this part of the economy by lessening the number of foreclosures. Those who invest in mortgage funds now can be sure that every property buyer must prove that he or she has a job and that the job will provide a sufficient salary to pay the mortgage payments. While borrowers may complain about being limited to mortgage monthly payments that are around 36% of their gross monthly income, those same borrowers will have some protection from the problems of foreclosure. And yes, this will result in fewer new homeowners.

For the landlord with property to rent this is a positive because with fewer people able to get financing for home purchases, more people will want to rent. In addition, when fewer people are able to get mortgages, sales of vacation homes drop, so those who rent out their vacation homes will have many more potential tenants to choose from.

WATCH INDUSTRY TRENDS

The renting industry is in a constant flux. Currently some of the hot topics are allowing pets, access for the disabled, enforcing rules regarding criminals/criminal activity, and keeping tenants safe.

✪   Allowing pets. For years the standard rental has decreed "No Pets," but that is changing. The country has become aware of the need for and importance of pets in the lives of many people. For the elderly a pet may be the only contact with a loved one. For a disabled child, a pet may be an important way to learn socialization. Animal support groups have done research showing that tenants with pets are more stable and more reliable than those who have not invested in a pet. The number of pet owners is growing and so is the number of landlords who allow pets.

✪   Access for the disabled. Not only is this a good idea, it is the law in many states, a law that is often abused. Tenant groups are a vocal lobby which can and does target landlords who do not provide such access. Along with the disabled, as the population ages, landlords are being urged to retrofit their property for the baby boomers who suffer from arthritis and other afflictions.

✪   Access and property designed for aging boomers. Sadly, the baby boomers are getting old. We are no longer going to be satisfied with that cute five-story walk-up in the artsy neighborhood. Our hips can barely go up five steps, let alone five stories. We are going to demand, and have the numbers and money to back-up our demands, that where we rent the building be equipped for us. This does not mean that we are old, it just means we need some assistance—like shower bars to help us in and out of the shower, wider doorways, no loose carpeting, and elevators—so that we can live normal lives. We will also expect a place to park our car, a clubhouse for our parties, and no screaming kids. The entry of the boomers into the senior rental market will bring major changes.

✪   Enforcing rules regarding criminals, criminal activity, and keeping tenants safe. In some government-funded housing units the landlord can be held liable for damage or injuries due to criminal activity if it can be proved that the landlord knew about the activity and did nothing. Some cities are taking that idea one step further to include *all* rental units, not just those receiving government funding. This is especially true in the larger cities that are concentrating on putting safety measures in place for rentals as a way to decrease crime. The courts are now looking harshly at landlords who neglect the simple protections such as proper lighting, locks, and other common safety measures.

SECTION 2

STYLES OF LANDLORDS AND GETTING HELP

We begin this section with a test to help you determine your style as a landlord. Once you find out what type of landlord you are, some suggestions are provided as to whom you should look to for assistance.

The rest of the section is all about getting help, exploring three potential sources: help from property managers, help from attorneys, and help from tradespeople.

What Type of Landlord Are You?

HOW MUCH DO YOU WANT TO BE INVOLVED?

One of the first decisions that a new landlord must make is how much he or she wants to be on site. There is no right or wrong answer to this; it is a personal preference. There are some considerations no matter what level of involvement you select. What type of landlord are you?

- **TYPE 1**—I purchased the property and I collect the rent, nothing more. This is merely an investment for me.

- **TYPE 2**—I no longer live in the same area/state as the rental property. While I want involvement beyond just banking the rent checks, I am not sure what I can do since I am both out of the area/state and tied to a job that takes up most of my free time.

- **TYPE 3**—Being a landlord is not my full-time job, but I want to be involved in some of the important things like screening potential tenants, overseeing expenses, and having the final say about any changes to the property.

✪   **TYPE 4**—I am renting out my family's home, which is very special to me. My concerns are protecting the home from damage so it can be sold at some time in the future, selecting tenants who will not abuse this property, and bringing in enough money to pay the bills on this property so it is not lost in a foreclosure. I don't know how to be a landlord; I have been thrown into this position and I am very uncomfortable.

✪   **TYPE 5**—I want to be involved with every aspect of being a landlord, BUT I am unsure how to proceed and I am not a handyman.

✪   **TYPE 6**—I purchased a multi-unit building so that I can live in the same building and have total, hands-on control over the rentals. I am fairly good at fixing things.

✪   **TYPE 7**—I have been a landlord for years. I think I know pretty much all there is to know about the profession. It is my livelihood and my passion. I may not be able to fix every problem but I have a network of professionals who can.

TYPE 1 and **TYPE 2** landlords should consider hiring a full-service property management company to handle their rental property. These full-service companies take over all the duties of being a landlord, from dealing with prospective tenants, to keeping up with repairs, to handling day-to-day problems, to legal evictions. Yes, the landlord pays for these services, but it allows the landlord to concentrate on other aspects of life, secure in the knowledge that the rental property is being handled in a professional and legal manner. There are property management companies throughout the United States; many are concentrated in the larger cities.

TYPE 2 and **TYPE 3** landlords should look at three options: 1) a property management company that will allow them to select only certain services; 2) a local real estate office that offers limited property management; and 3) hiring an experienced property manager who will live on the premises.

Many property management companies have branched out into what are termed *à la carte* services, where the landlord selects what services he or she wants to pay for. In addition, some of the major real estate offices have added property management services to their plate. Such an office may be a good fit for a landlord who has been unable to sell his or her property for a sufficient amount but may be willing to enter into a rent with an option to buy contract. Finally, the landlord may want to find an experienced property manager who can be on the premises full-time to handle problems and repairs. If the property is a multiple-unit building, the landlord may want to offer the property manager a salary and a place to live on premises as compensation.

TYPE 4, TYPE 5, TYPE 6, and **TYPE 7** landlords are more than likely not going to want to or be financially able to hire a property manager or a property management company. There is nothing negative about being your own property manager. In fact, it is the only way to make sure that things are done according to your standards and as economically as possible.

First-time landlords, take heart—you do have places to turn to for assistance. The first step in obtaining that assistance is getting this book. In this book we will direct you to both the obvious and the not-so-obvious places for help. For the experienced landlords we provide some new ideas and some more efficient ways to handle problems. All landlords who are going without a professional manager will need to build up a network of local people to help. We will discuss this further in future chapters.

Getting Help—
Property Managers

A landlord, especially someone who is a first-time landlord, may deal with several experts in renting out property. Even if you are planning to go it alone you may later change your mind about who you turn to for assistance. This chapter discusses the property manager expert that a landlord may want to retain.

PROPERTY MANAGERS AND PROPERTY MANAGEMENT COMPANIES

As we discussed, you need to determine how much control you want to have or are able to have over your rental property. As you are probably aware, there is much information and legal knowledge a hands-on landlord needs to have. If you have become a landlord as an investment, have several rental properties, or live out of state, it may be more cost-efficient to have an expert manage these properties than to attempt to manage them yourself. These experts are called property managers or property management companies.

The difference between a property manager and a property management company can be vast. Usually the property manager is one person who may or may not live on the premises. He or she has experience in managing other rentals and may have special education in property management. Property management companies are multi-person businesses who specialize in running properties for owners. If you have ever been in one of those large office buildings that hold many companies, you have been in a building that is run by a property management company. Property management companies can specialize in residential or business buildings.

Landlords who are on tight budgets, are living in the rental property, or want optimum control over the building may decide to do the management themselves. Before you make that decision read the rest of this chapter to see if you will be able to handle what a property manager is expected to handle.

PROS AND CONS OF HIRING A PROPERTY MANAGEMENT COMPANY

Pros
- All legal issues are handled correctly, and if there is a slip you may be able to get reimbursement from the property management company.

- The property is kept up to the requirements of the current laws.

- You are not subject to the complaints or criticisms of the tenants.

- The property upkeep is handled by professionals who can act before problems become disasters, and can negotiate contracts that will save you money.

- The property management company can handle pre-screening and background checks of all tenants.

- Evictions are handled by an independent entity in accordance with the local laws.

- A property management company can insulate you from the repercussions of bad press.

✪   A property management company can take care of rental listings that are aimed at a desirable audience.

✪   For a large, multi-rental building or for an owner who lives several states away a property management company is almost a necessity.

✪   Property management fees might qualify as a business expense deduction.

Cons   ✪   It is expensive to hire a property management company; that money may be better used in paying down the mortgage note on the property. Property Managers usually charge between 3 and 10 percent of the total rent, depending on the services provided.

✪   The level of service provided by a property management company may not be what you want or need.

✪   The property management company substitutes its judgment for yours, which may not be what you want.

✪   Any concerns you have about the property might go unaddressed during off-hours or on weekends.

PROS AND CONS OF HIRING A PROPERTY MANAGER

Pros   ✪   A property manager usually will live in the rental building and will be available for tenant disasters.

✪   You are only dealing with one person, the property manager, who is your employee and will follow your directions.

✪   For houses, the property manager might be a real estate professional (who does not live on the premises) who can not only work at keeping the property rented, but can ultimately work toward selling the property.

✪   A property manager may have a better, more personal relationship with the tenants that a property management company.

Cons   ✪   You may have problems with a property manager—poor work ethic, lack of ability, lack of experience, theft of rents, or any number of other issues.

✪   A property manager might not follow your directions.

✪   A property manager might use his or her position at the rental property to intimidate or bully tenants or, worse, to extort money in exchange for work.

HOW TO FIND A PROPERTY MANAGEMENT COMPANY OR PROPERTY MANAGER

Once you decide you want to hire a property management company or a property manager, your next task is finding the right one.

For a property management company you may want to go to the Internet and search for such a company in your area. Most property management companies have websites that contain information about their services. If you belong to a professional trade group, the group may be able to supply names of companies that have been screened for good service. Finding good property management companies is one of the benefits of membership. There are also landlord professional trade groups that screen and rank individual property managers.

You may find a good property management company by looking at other rental properties and finding out who manages them. You might also ask other landlords for referrals. And you can always go to the local telephone directories.

Another option is to use a real estate firm that will manage the property and may also list it for sale, including handling a lease with an option to buy.

Finding an individual to act as a property manager may be more difficult. Again, some landlord professional trade groups screen and rate such people. You may also be able to get some assistance from real estate professionals. One way to get the property manager that you want is to advertise for one, just as you do when hiring any other employee, after all the property manager is your employee. You can put an ad in the newspaper or list the job opening with a placement company. In these economic times when even multi-unit rentals are in foreclosure and many rental properties are going condominium, the availability of experienced property managers is up.

HOW TO HIRE A PROPERTY MANAGEMENT COMPANY OR PROPERTY MANAGER

The process of signing up with a property management company or a real estate firm is the same as the process of signing up with any professional. The landlord interviews several companies, looks at the differences in costs and services, and then selects a company that meets his or her needs. When doing the investigation the landlord may want to consult with organizations such as the Better Business Bureau or other business rating groups to see if there are any negative comments about a particular company.

When hiring an individual property manager you need to first decide what the duties of that property manager will be. This is the time to make a list of those items that the property manager *must* do, as well as things you would *like* the property manager to do.

Next you need to determine what compensation the property manager will be offered. It is not unusual for the property manager to receive a salary, a place to live in a multi-unit property, and reimbursement for expenses. As with any occupation, the more experience and expertise the property manager has, the higher the salary.

Finally, you need to interview prospective property managers to see who will fit the criteria and who can best handle the property. The landlord should use the same tools for screening a property manager as for screening prospective tenants: check references, do a background check, and contact former employers. Again, you can have a placement company handle the screenings and first-round eliminations.

LANDLORD'S LIABILITY FOR PROPERTY MANAGEMENT COMPANIES OR PROPERTY MANAGERS

The landlord may have very little legal liability for what employees of a property management company or a real estate firm do when handling your account. Much of the liability is controlled by the contract between the landlord and the property management company. In general terms, you probably will not be responsible for negligence on the part of the property management company *if* you take steps to stop the negligence as soon as you are made aware of it. Here the landlord is dealing with the mistakes/errors/negligence of an employee of the property management company. Applying common agency law, the property management company holds the brunt of the responsibility for its employee assigned to the landlord's account. As with everything else, the liability is controlled by local laws.

A landlord typically has much more liability for the mistakes/errors/negligence of an individual property manager. In this case, the property manager is your employee and legally considered your agent. Under agency law, the acts of the agent are also the acts of the principle. Because the property manager is an employee, the landlord has the usual legal liability that employers have for the actions of their employees when the employee is acting within the scope of his or her job responsibilities.

Looking at this as strict liability, you definitely have more exposure or liability if you hire an individual as a property manager than if you sign with a property management company or real estate firm.

ENDING THE RELATIONSHIP WITH A PROPERTY MANAGEMENT COMPANY OR PROPERTY MANAGER

It happens in just about every client or employment relationship: there comes a point when the client or employer must end the relationship. If the landlord has hired a property management company or real estate firm, the parting will probably come at the end of the contract that you signed with the property management company or real estate firm. It is a business deal that has run its term. No hard feelings, no explanations needed.

It is a whole other issue when the landlord needs to terminate a property manager, who is an employee. If you have decided to hire the property manager using an employment contract, the contract *must* contain information as to how to end that contract. Perhaps you have given the property manager a yearly contract, which must be renewed every year. In that case, the contract ends when you do not renew the contract.

Problems can arise when a property manager is hired, as most employees are hired, as an "at will" employee who can be terminated for anything except discrimination (see www.eeoc.gov). In this case the landlord must be careful to follow both local and federal employment laws. This book cannot contain all the information that an employer needs regarding terminating an employee. Please look at www.sphinxlegal.com for more books that address this topic. I, of course, would recommend my book on employment law, which can be found at this address.

Getting Help— Attorneys

In this chapter we discuss the one person that every landlord will eventually go to for help, an attorney. The type of attorney used by a landlord will primarily practice in the areas of landlord/tenant law or real estate law, or civil rights law for rental discrimination cases. Landlords and property owners go to attorneys to tell them what the law is where the property is located, for representation in a sale or purchase, to negotiate with others, to represent them in court, and to create documents that will keep them out of court.

CAN I BE SUED?

To every lawyer, "Can I be sued?" is a common question. Many a phone conversation with a potential client begins this way. The short answer is yes; in today's litigious society anyone can sue anyone for anything. Thus, the more important question is, "Will the lawsuit against me be successful?" Success or failure in a lawsuit depends on the law and the ability of your representative—your attorney.

WHAT CAN AN ATTORNEY DO FOR ME?

Landlord/tenant laws can be complex, especially when the landlord has to deal with local ordinances and building codes. For that reason many landlords turn to attorneys for assistance, sometimes even before they make the decision to rent out their property. Many potential landlords will have an attorney review the law in a particular area before they make an offer to purchase property to be rented out.

Sometimes a landlord can get into a situation that requires a court appearance. This can be in conjunction with changing a zoning ordinance, the removal of a tenant, or in a suit against a former tenant. Landlords can also find themselves in court responding to allegations of not complying with certain laws or as a third party who is brought in because of an incident at the rental property. As our laws become more complex it is becoming more commonplace for landlords to hire an attorney to draw up legal documents and give advice on how to comply with the law.

As a rental property owner it is almost a guarantee that you will need an attorney to assist you regarding your rental property at some point. It may be your first experience with the legal system—a system that is complex, slow, and at times may seem unfair.

WHERE CAN I FIND AN ATTORNEY?

The first step to find an attorney who can help you is to ask friends, family, your landlord association, the chamber of commerce where your property is located, your banker, and your business acquaintances for a referral. Another way to find an attorney is through a local bar association. There are hundreds of bar associations in the United States. Not all states require licensed attorneys to belong to a particular bar association; however, most attorneys are members of at least one country, state, county, city, or type of practice bar association. These associations usually have some type of attorney referral plan to match the public with their members. Because landlord/tenant law is state-specific you should look for an attorney who is licensed in your state.

Finally, when looking for a lawyer you can do an Internet search on terms like "landlord/tenant law," "landlord attorney," "evictions," etc., plus your state. Such a search will bring up a variety of law firms' and attorneys' websites. Being able to read about a law firm or an attorney via their websites is the most helpful way to determine if this attorney can help you.

WHEN DO I NEED AN ATTORNEY?

Rules of thumb are that you hire an attorney:

1. when the other side hires an attorney;

2. when you are being brought into court for not complying with civil rights laws;

3. when you are the third party in a suit brought due to an incident between a tenant and another party;

4. when you have already lost at a preliminary hearing in front of city/town authorities on this same matter;

5. when the amount you are being sued for will cause you to go into bankruptcy; or

6. when you feel that you are overwhelmed with the legal procedure.

Occasionally I will have a potential client come to me after he or she has attempted to act as his or her own attorney. In the majority of those situations, the non-attorney has inadvertently complicated things so much that it will take many more attorney work hours that the client must pay for, in order to straighten things out and then to resolve the matter, than it would have taken to simply resolve the matter if an attorney had been hired right away. What is even worse is sometimes the person who acted as his or her own attorney has done legal damage that an attorney cannot repair. It is always less expensive for the client to hire an attorney at the beginning of a problem than to hire the attorney after the problem has been complicated.

HOW TO GET WHAT YOU WANT FROM AN ATTORNEY

You may want to find out more about an attorney before hiring that person. You can do this by looking at the online listings for this attorney. Does he or she have a website? Is he or she listed in any of the common legal references? Next, call the attorney. In that initial phone call you will be able to determine if this attorney can assist you. If you cannot speak with the attorney directly, do not hesitate to ask the office staff if that law office handles your type of case.

On the initial call the attorney will probably ask you lots of questions about your case. The attorney wants to see if you are within the proper time limits to proceed with the case, if you are in the right area of law, and if the case is something that the attorney can help you with. Most attorneys will explain how their particular law firm works in terms of billing, time limits, and law firm policies. If this attorney can help you and if you think this is the person you want to represent you, the next step may be a face-to-face meeting. If time limits are tight, you may be able to do much of the work via phone, fax, and e-mail. Common examples of this are cases where the hearing date is rapidly approaching and certain documents are needed, or if the attorney is only reviewing agreements.

Bring all your documents to your attorney. It is best to make copies of these documents first and provide the attorney with the copies (that way you always have the originals). Bring your questions and a pad of paper to take notes on what the attorney will do. Make sure that you understand how the attorney will be billing you.

WAYS TO GET THE MOST WORK OUT OF YOUR ATTORNEY

1. Pay the bill. If you feel you may have problems with money, that should be discussed with the attorney up front. Make sure you know how the bill is calculated before you sign on with an attorney.

2. Make the most out of any time you have with your attorney. When you speak with your attorney (on the phone or in person), have your questions ready, your documents in front of you, and a pen to write down the answers you are given.

3. Be respectful. Leave the lawyer jokes, stories about how some lawyer ripped off your friend, and negative comments about the legal profession at home.

4. Take the advice of your attorney. Doing something that is against your attorney's advice and then calling the attorney to help you out of your self-made problem inevitably results in a higher bill because of the extra work. There are times when even the best attorney cannot fix a problem that a client has gotten himself or herself into.

5. Be honest with your attorney. Remember that everything you discuss with your attorney is legally held in confidence due to attorney-client privilege. If you are not honest with your attorney, the attorney cannot fully assist you in your case. Your attorney cannot fully represent you unless he or she knows all the facts, even the ones that make you look guilty.

ATTORNEY'S FEES

Attorneys vary in what they charge and how they charge. Not all attorneys make the big money that is portrayed on TV. Because of the huge increase in number of licensed attorneys, the majority of attorneys are merely pulling in a middle-class salary. Like the rest of the population they must get paid in order to support their family. A law license does not come with free gasoline, free utilities, or free food. No lawyer wants to find out that a client scammed him or her out of legitimate fees for work that has been done.

Understand that getting paid is just as important to the attorney as it is to you. If you have financial issues, it is best to bring them up when you first speak with your attorney. The majority of attorneys are more than happy to work with a client on a budget, as long as that client is honest about the need. There are times when an attorney can make certain adjustments, for example taking on only a part of a case, such as just the mediation, in order to keep the bill down. You can also offer to do some of the legwork on the case, such as picking up documents, running documents to the court, etc.

Attorneys charge by an hourly rate, a flat fee, a contingency, or any combination of these. An hourly rate is the most common way that attorneys bill. That amount is usually in line with what other attorneys in the same area and with the same experience charge. A flat fee is a new way that some attorneys will bill instead of the hourly rate. When charging a flat fee, the attorney has averaged or estimated how long a particular task will take, and has set as the flat fee that average or estimate. Most attorneys ask for the flat fee up front, although that varies by case. The good news for the client is that an attorney is more than likely giving the client a break on the price when using a flat fee.

A contingency fee is when the client pays for expenses and the attorney only gets money if the client wins. At that point the attorney gets a percentage of the winnings. Not all cases can be done on contingency because not all cases will have settlements. For example, in an eviction there is no settlement, so attorneys cannot charge a contingency fee.

Attorneys are not required to bill in a particular manner, so you will see many combinations of billings. Many attorneys will ask for a retainer (an amount up front) that they will bill against. Once the retainer gets below a certain dollar amount, the client will be required to replenish that amount.

The other way of billing that clients want to know about is *pro bono*, meaning "for free." In today's economy it is almost impossible for attorneys to take on free cases unless they are in a big firm that does charity work. There are legal aid groups who do take cases on for little or no money. However, in most cases the client must prove by IRS statements that he or she is unable to pay. Law schools sometimes provide a certain amount of free legal work, as do many community groups. If you are already getting state aid the office providing that aid may be able to assist you in finding free legal work. You can also call your local bar associations for that type of referral.

SCREENING ATTORNEYS

It is more than understandable that when a person is looking for an attorney he or she will call several law firms to get information and find the perfect fit. That is being a good consumer. Most attorneys are glad to speak with a person who needs information, and many may even direct the caller to another attorney who better fits the caller's needs. Attorneys who offer free telephone consultations may speak with over one hundred people in a week, many of whom merely need direction or a question answered.

Sometimes the person who needs the attorney is not the person calling the attorney. Many attorneys have been contacted by a spouse or family member of a person who allegedly needs legal assistance only to find out that the person neither wants nor will accept the help of an attorney. That wastes everyone's time and effort. Also, in these phone conversations the lawyer needs to ask detailed questions about the facts to see if there is a case that can go into court. If the person who needs the attorney is not on the phone it not only wastes time but can result in the attorney being given the wrong information.

So, please call several attorneys before you make your decision, and do the calling yourself.

ENDING THE ATTORNEY/CLIENT RELATIONSHIP

If it happens that the attorney you selected does not do what you wanted him or her to do, or if you just do not want to deal with that person for future legal issues, you can end the attorney/client relationship. The best way to do this is to speak with the attorney and explain the problem. If you have not paid your bill, expect the attorney to insist that you pay up before he or she bows out of the case.

In the majority of landlord/tenant cases the attorney does a transaction for the client, payment is made, and the attorney goes on to the next client. It is rare for these types of cases to languish on for years and years. Nevertheless, it is always a good idea to have an attorney you can call upon for advice when dealing with legal problems, even if your current problem is not in the attorney's area of expertise. Most attorneys value their former clients and are more than happy to help them find another attorney for different types of law.

Getting Help—Tradespeople

Tradespeople are the professionals who keep your building running. They are the plumber, the heating/air conditioning repair person, the electrician, the painter, the decorator, the bricklayer, anyone whose job it is to keep your rental building running. Why are these people so important? Because without competent tradespeople the landlord is the one who has to snake out the toilet when it backs up in the middle of the night, or repair the wiring when the electricity goes out. Think of tradespeople as your repair staff who are only paid when they work.

WHO ARE TRADESWORKERS, AND WHERE CAN I FIND THEM?

Tradesworkers or tradespeople are those who we call upon to do the blue collar work around our property. Yes, I can hear you now saying, "I do everything myself." That is great, that is the way to save money. But what happens when the task is beyond your expertise, like putting in a new furnace or rewiring a home or getting new electrical service from the pole to your property? Face it; we all have to call upon the experts for things like this.

I will also share a secret with my readers, as a person who always wanted to do everything myself: I have come to a point where hiring a professional to do nasty chores like mowing the lawn and plowing the snow off my driveway is great. It leaves me with more time to do what I enjoy without grousing about my sore back or hurting muscles.

Finding someone to do minor or major repairs is yet another adventure. You can ask friends, colleagues, and other landlords, or look on the Internet. There are some services that evaluate workers and help people get the type of worker they need. You can also look at the Better Business Bureau website, Angie's list, or one of the landlord association websites.

I find many good workers through my local newspaper, which sells ads at the back of the paper. I also use the local phone book for my city. It seems that those who are invested in my town because they live here or have a business here are reliable. Finally, the best tradespeople that I have found are those whose names I got from other satisfied customers. Word of mouth is absolutely the very best advertising that any business can get.

CHECKING REFERENCES

When you hire a trades-person to work on your property you should do some checking. For certain professions the business needs to be licensed and may need to be certified by a local trade association. These are things that are good to know. My mom once hired a person to repair the bricks on her home; when the repair fell apart she was able to get a quick and thorough repair through the local bricklayers association in her city. So it is important to at least note the credentials for the worker and his or her business.

I prefer looking at the business using the existing tools on the Internet. I look at the business's website. What are they saying about their own work? Do they have guarantees? Do they provide information that you need? Are they certified by any organization? I also look at the state website to see if the company is incorporated with the state. What do the state papers say? Is the person who says he or she is the owner listed on the corporate papers, or is this person merely in sales? I ask questions of tradesworkers before I hire them, like what will they do if I am unhappy with the work. I want to know how much satisfaction I can get and how fast. Finally I look at the Better Business Bureau to see if the company has any charges against them.

Do you need to do a full detective-style background check on every worker who enters your property? Probably not, especially if you found this person through a referral from another property owner. This type of investigation should be limited to employees, since this type of background check takes time and money.

Are there places where a landlord can get a simple background/credit check? Yes, many of the national landlord associations include this type of service for their members. If this is important to you, it will undoubtedly be less expensive if you can get this service from an association than it will be if you pay for each background check through an investigative agency.

MAINTENANCE CONTRACT OR EMERGENCY USE

The worst time to judge the ability of workers is during an emergency call. I have met what turned out to be excellent plumbers, electricians, and furnace repair people in the middle of cold holiday nights. Nevertheless, the best time to evaluate a tradesworker is during the day when you have him or her come in to do a check, a once-over, or a simple task.

If you want to begin your relationship with one of these no-stress meetings, you may want to have an initial checkup call where the tradesperson goes over your building and provides you with an evaluation of the current status and potential flaws in your system. Many people will have a heating/air conditioning company come out in spring and in fall to go over the entire system, check for possible flaws, and get the furnace/air conditioner ready for the upcoming season. These are considered maintenance calls.

As a landlord you may want to make sure that your favorite tradesperson is available whenever you call, so you sign a contract with that person. These contracts can include certain standard maintenance, or maybe even a lower cost on emergency calls. The landlord gets two benefits from this: 1) preventative maintenance may avoid massive breakdowns; and 2) being under contract puts you at the top of the list when many people are trying to get service.

Depending on the size of the rental property and the area where the property is located, a landlord may want to do some pre-need arrangements with trade businesses. This is especially true in areas where tradesworkers are kept busy and new customers may be put to the back of the line. Pre-need arrangements are a way to introduce the landlord and the building to these businesses. The landlord may want to open an account with a trade business so that those middle-of-the-night calls can be handled quickly.

BUILDING A NETWORK OF TRADESWORKERS

Landlords, like all property owners, need to have a network of professionals that can be called on to handle repairs on plumbing, electrical, gas, heating, and cooling, as well as general repairs. Every landlord should build a network of professionals that can be called upon to handle these issues. There are several ways to build this network.

- ✪ If the landlord has signed with a property management company, this chore may be handled by this company, depending on the agreement.

- ✪ Landlords who become members of professional landlord organizations may be able to obtain lists of local workers as part of the benefits of belonging to that organization.

- ✪ Landlords may be able to obtain referrals from other landlords in the area or through real estate professionals.

- ✪ Experienced property managers may come with their own set of tradesworkers who can be called upon to handle a job.

- ✪ Finally, the landlord can ask friends and family for referrals. But before calling one of these make sure to check them out with the Better Business Bureau (www.bbb.org) or with local business rating services.

ENDING A RELATIONSHIP WITH A TRADESWORKER

The good thing about creating and keeping your network of tradespeople up to date is that you will always be able to find someone to do the job you need done. There may come a time when the tradesworker that you have called on for many years is no longer doing a competent job or when you simply want to try a new system. The separation should be relatively simple and painless. Just make sure that you are not contractually obligated to a particular trades-person or his or her business. Once the contract is ended you are free to select another trades-person to handle the job.

Do not be surprised if your former worker and your new worker know each other and have swapped stories about their customers. For the landlord or homeowner it can be a bit disconcerting when your current electrician says he or she knows your former electrician and asks why you stopped using the other person's service. Be honest. Something like, "I picked your firm because the other firm made me wait for service calls," or "I wanted to try your service so more than one worker would understand my A/C system," is a perfectly acceptable response. These rather awkward moments are not the time for personal assessments like, "He had body odor." Keep your comments to just business.

Finally, and we have all done it, some of us many times, we may hire a new business to handle a job that a previous business was doing just fine because of that discount ticket in the mail or because we were just bored. We hire the new business and then find out they are just not as good as the previous workers were. Then we need to make nice with the previous business.

I did this with a central air conditioning unit. My usual A/C repair person could fix any problem, he knew my very fussy A/C unit like the back of his hand. Then one day I got a really good discount ad for A/C repair and called the new guy. Well, the new guy ended up making things so much worse that by the end of the day the A/C refused to even turn on.

I then had to make that horrid "I goofed" phone call to the usual repairman. The misery of eating crow! Yes, I did apologize for letting someone else work on the unit. I praised my A/C repairman and his ability to fix just about anything. And, after many hours, he was indeed able to repair the repairs I had bought with that discount coupon. The discount ended up costing me dearly.

SECTION 3

LAWS THAT IMPACT LANDLORDS

This section is my favorite, since it is all about the laws. We start with state and local laws, then go into the much more complex area of federal laws and laws about hazards and toxicity. This section shows you where you can find these laws and what happens if someone accuses you of breaking one of these laws.

State and Local Laws

This chapter is about the laws and rules that will have the most effect on you and your property—local and state laws. These can be the little things that will stop you in your tracks because they are unique to your city. It would be impossible to list all these laws, but this chapter provides some basic information on how to find these local laws.

THE BASICS—CAN YOUR PROPERTY BE LEGALLY RENTED?

Before you hang that For Rent sign on the outside of your property you will need to do some homework to see if you can actually rent out your property. That's right, even if you legally own the property and want to legally rent the property to perfectly good tenants you may be prevented from doing so, or you may be required to make so many changes that it is cheaper to let the property sit empty.

There are three things that may stop you from renting the property. They are: 1) local association rules; 2) local city/county laws; and 3) state laws. We will discuss federal laws and their effect on your property later. Federal laws are directed at not being discriminatory in renting and at safety hazards in the building. For the most part, the biggest problems for the landlord will come from the three local entities listed above.

LOCAL ASSOCIATION RULES

If your property is in a gated community, part of a cooperative association, part of a condominium association, or part of a local homeowners association, you may not have the authority to rent out your property. The association may bar tenants or may require that you and the tenant qualify or pay extra for the right to rent out your own property.

These are the issues that make normally calm people livid. After long research you purchased a piece of property. One of the benefits of that property was an active and protective association. You gladly paid the assessments to the association because you got so much out of it. The association supplied security, groundskeeping, maintenance of common areas, laundry rooms and party rooms, a community exercise center, and handled the property in accordance with the wishes of the owners. All of which saved you money. To you the association was a very positive element—until you decided to be a landlord.

That same association may now turn into your principal foe in your efforts to rent out your property. Many associations, especially condominium and cooperative associations where the property shares common walls, have rules that prohibit or greatly reduce the value of renting the property. The reason is simple: when the real estate boom hit, many apartment building owners turned their buildings into condominiums or cooperatives. Some of the new owners decided that they could make money by renting their units, and a lack of proper tenant screening brought problems.

Responses to the tenant problems were new rules about renting. These associations, because they had the legal authority to make their own rules, wrote rules that went from barring tenants, to charging extra for renting out the property, to requiring approval of tenants by the association, and more. The goal was to keep people who did not have a stake in the property from living there. In some cases these rules worked, and in others they didn't, leading to still more changes in the rules.

Please note that if you own a vacation home that has an association, your association may require that they do the listing and renting in a time-share method. For many owners of vacation homes this requirement is really a service. It allows those who do not live close to the rental to leave the cleaning, marketing, and screening of tenants up to the professionals. We will offer more information on vacation home rentals in another chapter.

If your property belongs to any association, the first thing you need to do is to look at the association agreement that you signed when you purchased the property, plus the updates. Don't have a current agreement? Get a copy from the association office. You can ask someone in the association office about renting, but be careful—sometimes those who staff these offices are not completely familiar with the fine print of the agreement. If you want to rent your property you need solid information which is built upon the agreement you signed. Also, you may want to pursue legal action to modify or break the agreement, and for that you will need to present the agreement to your attorney.

Once you have the agreement you will need to go through each word to see if the issue of renting is addressed. Yes, this is tedious work—work that you can pay your attorney to do for you. That said, I suggest that you at least try to work through a reading of this agreement. Not only do you want to search for any language about renting, you will also want to look for rules that are not being enforced and rules that are being enforced inconsistently.

If you do proceed into litigation your attorney will want to know if the association is not enforcing some of the rules or is only enforcing the rules on certain people. There have been several court cases against associations that enforced rules in a way that discriminated against a particular race. Such acts can be considered discrimination under both state and federal laws.

LOCAL CITY/COUNTY/STATE LAWS

WARNING! WARNING! Your city, county, and state laws may make it prohibitively expensive to turn your property into a rental. The laws of your area may require very expensive changes to your property in order for it to be used as a legal rental. As a landlord you must know the local laws that will affect your rental property.

Example of a Law That Would Change How You Rent

In a Midwest town the law requires that each apartment have two doors that exit to the outside, with those doors on different sides of the building. Tim owns a large older home that has a fully furnished second floor, first floor, and basement. If Tim wants to separate this house into three different apartments he will need to make structural changes including additional stairways and doors at the top and the basement levels. Tim has a contractor give him an estimate of the cost of the work and decides it is just too expensive, so he decides to rent out the entire house to one tenant.

Tim also has to deal with a law that requires that rented properties must have a minimum of two parking spots, off the city street, for each tenant. For this Tim adds a long carport that is attached to the garage. The carport provides a paved slab where two additional cars can park.

Finding the Law

Begin by making sure you know what town, city, township, county, and state your rental property is in. Sounds silly? Many landlords are shocked to find that their property is on the border of a particular city/county/state line and the laws they were following do not apply.

The first step in preparing your property to rent is to do your homework on the laws in your area. For that begin with what your city/county/state has online in the way of laws. (See Appendix A.) If you cannot easily figure out what changes, if any, are required to make your building a rental, contact your local building department. Building departments are usually the ones enforcing the laws so they may have some great suggestions.

You may also want to begin a relationship with an attorney who handles landlord/tenant cases. You will use this attorney in several matters regarding being a landlord such as drafting the lease, evictions, and possibly defending against housing discrimination charges, so it is a good idea to find an attorney who can assist you right from the start. You can also turn your rental over to a property management company which will have the answers to all these questions.

chapter 8

Federal Laws

This chapter discusses the many federal laws that have an effect on the landlord/tenant relationship. These are not the only laws that the landlord needs to be aware of. In Appendix A we have listed, by state, the state landlord/tenant statutes. Your county and city may also have laws that will impact a rental. If the rental property is located in a gated community or a community that has an association, the landlord must also abide by the association rules on rentals.

FEDERAL LAWS

✪ **Fair Housing Act**—Title VIII of the *Civil Rights Act of 1968* (42 U.S.C. §§ 3601–19, 3631) prohibits discrimination in the sale, rental, and financing of housing based on race, color, national origin, religion, sex, familial status (including children under the age of 18 living with parents of legal custodians and pregnant women), and disability.

LINK: www.usdoj.gov/crt/housing/title8.htm

The victim of discrimination can file a civil suit, a Housing and Urban Development (HUD) complaint, or request that the local U.S. Attorney General prosecute those convicted of a violation. Damages can include actual loss and punitive damages. Failure to participate in the suit or complaint by refusing to produce records can result in a fine and/or prison time.

These laws prohibit housing discrimination against people have a mental or physical disability which limits one or more life actions, those who have a history of disability, and/or those who are regarded by others as having a disability. Disabilities mentioned are hearing loss, loss of mobility, visual impairments, mental illness, AIDS, HIV, and mental retardation. However, this law is not limited to these specific disabilities.

Landlords are required to evaluate a disabled potential tenant on the same financial stability and history criteria that are used to evaluate all other prospective tenants. (This is one of many good reasons for landlords to keep detailed records on potential tenant evaluations.) Landlords cannot question the severity of a disability or require a disabled person to produce his or her medical records.

Landlords must accommodate the reasonable needs of disabled tenants at the landlord's expense (42 U.S.C. § 3604(f) (3) (B)). Accommodations include handicapped parking (required by the laws of almost every state), a large parking space for wheelchair access, or other reasonably easy changes. Landlords are not required to go into major expenses such as installing an elevator in a building. However, some courts have found that installing an inexpensive concrete ramp for access to an entrance door is reasonable.

Disabled tenants must be allowed to make reasonable modifications to their own living units or common areas at the tenant's expense if the modification is necessary for the tenant to live comfortably and safely (42 U.S.C. § 3604(f) (3) (A)). These modifications must be: 1) reasonable; 2) needed for the comfort/ safety of the tenant; and 3) items that will not make the unit unacceptable for the next tenant or that will be restored to the original condition.

Landlords should require written descriptions of the modifications and proof that the work will be done in a safe, legal manner and will adhere to all local building code ordinances. The landlord should also request proof that the modification will address the disabled tenant's needs.

If the modifications proposed are such that the landlord will require the tenant to restore the premises, the landlord can require that the tenant put funds into an interest-bearing escrow account that will be used to pay for the restoration. The cost of the modification is legally the responsibility of the tenant, but if the modification is something that will remain after the disabled tenant leaves most landlords will assume a portion of the cost.

Some exceptions to this law do exist, especially for the owner who rents out his or her home because it is not selling. Also, your state laws may modify or completely change these requirements.

- ✪ **Fair Housing Act/Tenant Rights**—These laws are explained by the Department of Housing and Urban Development (HUD). The HUD website provides the most recent updates to federal housing laws:

  LINK: www.hud.gov/offices/fheo/FHLaws/yourrights.cfm

- ✪ **Title VI of the Civil Rights Act of 1964**—Title VI prohibits discrimination on the basis of race, color, or national origin in programs and housing that benefits from certain federal financial assistance.

  LINK: www.usdoj.gov/crt/grants_statutes/titlevi.txt

- ✪ *The Rehabilitation Act of 1973*—This act has several sections that may impact a landlord who is involved with HUD. These sections are:

- **Section 502:** created the U.S. Architectural and Transportation Barriers Compliance Board to ensure effective enforcement of the *Architectural Barriers Act of 1968.*

- **Section 503:** covers contractors who are hired by the federal government.

- **Section 504:** provides for nondiscrimination in all programs, services and activities, including housing, that receive federal financial assistance, and in programs, services, and activities conducted by executive agencies.

- **Section 505:** provides that the rights, remedies and procedures available under Title VI of the Civil Rights Act of 1964 shall be available to individuals who wish to file a complaint under Section 504. In addition, Section 505 allows for the award of attorney's fees for the prevailing party.

Technically, Section 504 prohibits discrimination based on disability in any program or activity receiving federal financial assistance. The act requires that reasonable accommodations be made to provide people with disabilities access to commercial premises. It forbids discrimination against the disabled by mandating access in commercial buildings.

LINK: www.usdoj.gov/crt/grants_statutes/titlevi.txt

- **Americans with Disabilities Act 1990 (ADA)**—Title II prohibits discrimination based on disability in programs, services, and activities provided or made available by public entities. HUD enforces Title II when it relates to state and local public housing, housing assistance, and housing referrals.

The ADA requires reasonable accommodations only if that accommodation can be achieved without undue burden or hardship to the landlord. For example, the ADA may require a certain number of handicapped parking places, wheelchair access from parking lots into buildings, and wider doors for access into commercial premises. The ADA does not usually cover residential property unless the property also includes public areas or if the property receives some financial federal benefit.

LINK: www.ada.gov/pubs/ada.htm

✪ **Section 109 of Title I of the *Housing and Community Development Act of 1974*** (Title I) (42 U.S.C. 5309)—Section 109 prohibits discrimination on the basis of race, color, national origin, sex, or religion in programs and activities receiving financial assistance from HUD's Community Development and Block Grant Program.

LINK: www.hud.gov/offices/fheo/FHLaws/109.cfm

✪ **Architectural Barriers Act of 1968**—The Architectural Barriers Act requires that buildings and facilities designed, constructed, altered, or leased with certain federal funds after September 1969 must be accessible to and usable by handicapped persons.

LINK: www.access-board.gov/about/laws/ABA.htm

NOTE: *In doing Internet searches on Federal housing / renting laws you are bound to come up with laws that are referred to as **model** or **uniform**. These are entire statutes that were written by an interested third party, such as a commission in a federal department or a legal group. The model or uniform statute is the result of many, many hours of research and work undertaken to produce something that is inclusive for all instances. However, until a state or the federal government officially adopts this model or uniform statute it is not law. In research for this book I found many model or uniform statutes that were labeled as landlord/tenant laws but that needed to have a state ratify the document into the state's legal system.*

As a landlord you should only be interested in what is actual law, not what could be. Concentrate your legal research on the state, the county, and the city where the rental property is located. If your state has adopted one of these model or uniform documents, it will be in your state's law access. Go to Appendix A for a list of the state laws.

Laws about Specific Hazards

This chapter covers the three hazards—lead-based paint, asbestos, and mold—that are addressed by both state and federal laws. The primary hazard is the issue of lead-based paint, which was previously used on many buildings that are now being rented out. Lead-based paint has been proven to harm children who ingest the paint chips. These hazards are the focus of many government agencies that can impact rentals.

HAZARDS COVERED BY FEDERAL REGULATIONS

Lead-Based Paint

Landlords may be liable for lead-based paint exposure. This occurs when the property has been painted with lead-based paint, which was common for years, and the paint is now chipping. The chips become a magnet to children, who put the paint chips in their mouths and absorb the lead. The prevention required is simple upkeep of all painted areas, particularly scraping away old paint and repainting. In addition, there are some newer types of paint that can decrease the instance of lead exposure when applied over lead-based paint.

Lead-based paint exposure on a rental property can also happen when the property is renovated, especially when other tenants continue to reside in attached units during the renovations. The landlord needs to check with the NLIC and EPA prior to starting any renovations on buildings that were built before 1978. The EPA requires that sixty days prior to renovations, current tenants be given information regarding lead-based paint dangers. This can usually be handled with a notice regarding the renovation's location and date, along with an EPA pamphlet on lead-based paint dangers.

Lead-based paint is not the only danger in renovations. Property owners may be liable for problems caused by exposure to other dangerous substances, especially during a renovation. One such substance is asbestos, discussed in more detail below. Regulations issued by the Occupational Safety and Health Administration (OSHA) set very strict standards for testing, maintenance, and disclosure of asbestos in buildings constructed prior to 1981. Many local communities have added regulations on asbestos through their building code ordinances. For information contact your local OSHA office or visit **www.osha.gov.**

Rental property that was built prior to 1978 is subject to the *Residential Lead-Based Paint Hazard Act*—Title X in the Environmental Protection Agency regulations (40 C.F.R. 745). This regulation requires a landlord in a property that qualifies under this act to give every tenant the EPA pamphlet "Protect Your Family From Lead In Your Home" or a state-approved local version of this pamphlet. Tenants are also required to sign an EPA disclosure form stating that they were informed about lead-based paint dangers.

For EPA disclosure forms, pamphlets, and information on lead-based paint liability contact:

EPA at www.epa.gov for your local EPA office

National Lead Information Center (NLIC)
1-800-424-LEAD (5323)
801 Roeder Road, Suite 600
Silver Spring, MD 20910
www.epa.gov/lead/nlic.htm

The following rental properties are not covered by this rule:

- ✪ housing which began construction after January 1, 1978;

- ✪ housing that has been certified as lead-free;

- ✪ lofts, efficiencies, and studio apartments;

- ✪ vacation rentals of one-hundred days or less;

- ✪ a single room rented in a residential home; and

- ✪ housing designed for those with disabilities or seniors, unless children under 6 years old are expected to live in the unit.

If you have any questions as to whether your property is covered, contact the EPA or NLIC.

Asbestos The best place to locate information on asbestos is at **www.epa.gov/asbestos/.** This is the EPA website that is devoted to asbestos—why it is a problem, and how to deal with it. Your state may also have laws or regulations about asbestos.

For example, in many cities a person who is demolishing a home that was built prior to 1960 must have water pouring onto the materials being demolished to prevent asbestos fibers from becoming airborne.

A landlord will probably encounter asbestos in the structure of an older property. Here is the EPA's list of common asbestos products in the home:

- ✪ **Steam pipes, boilers, and furnace ducts** insulated with an asbestos blanket or asbestos paper tape. These materials may release asbestos fibers if damaged, repaired, or removed improperly.

- ✪ **Resilient floor tiles** (vinyl asbestos, asphalt, and rubber), the backing on **vinyl sheet flooring,** and **adhesives** used for installing floor tile. Sanding tiles can release fibers. So can scraping or sanding the backing of sheet flooring during removal.

- ✪ **Cement sheet, millboard,** and **paper** used as insulation around furnaces and wood-burning stoves. Repairing or removing appliances can release asbestos fibers. So can cutting, tearing, sanding, drilling, or sawing insulation.

- ✪ **Door gaskets** in furnaces, wood stoves, and coal stoves. Worn seals can release asbestos fibers during use.

- ✪ **Soundproofing or decorative material** sprayed on walls and ceilings. Loose, crumbly, or water-damaged material may release fibers. So will sanding, drilling, or scraping the material.

- ✪ **Patching and joint compounds** for walls and ceilings, and **textured paints,** which were banned in 1977. Sanding, scraping, or drilling these surfaces may release asbestos.

- ✪ **Asbestos cement roofing, shingles,** and **siding.** These products are not likely to release asbestos fibers unless sawed, drilled, or cut.

- ✪ **Insulation** on houses built between 1930 and 1950 may contain asbestos. Attic and wall insulation produced using vermiculite ore, particularly ore that originated from a Libby, Montana mine, may contain asbestos fibers.

- ✪ **Artificial ashes** and **embers** sold for use in gas-fired fireplaces. Also, other older household products such as **fireproof gloves, stove-top pads, ironing board covers,** and certain **hair dryers.**

Asbestos Dos and Don'ts for the Homeowner from the EPA

- ✪ Do keep activities to a minimum in any areas having damaged material that may contain asbestos.

- ✪ Do take every precaution to avoid damaging asbestos material.

- ✪ Do have removal and major repair done by people trained and qualified in handling asbestos. It is highly recommended that sampling and minor repair also be done by asbestos professionals.

✪   Don't dust, sweep, or vacuum debris that may contain asbestos.

✪   Don't saw, sand, scrape, or drill holes in asbestos materials.

✪   Don't use abrasive pads or brushes on power strippers to strip wax from asbestos flooring. Never use a power stripper on a dry floor.

✪   Don't sand or try to level asbestos flooring or its backing. When asbestos flooring needs replacing, install new floor covering over it, if possible.

✪   Don't track material that could contain asbestos through the house. If you cannot avoid walking through the area, have it cleaned with a wet mop. If the material is from a damaged area, or if a large area must be cleaned, call an asbestos professional.

✪   Major repairs must be done only by a professional trained in methods for safely handling asbestos.

For more information on asbestos go to **www.epa.gov/asbestos.**

Mold   The EPA also has a lot of information on mold on its website at **www. epa.gov/mold/index.html.** Many of the federal laws concerning mold deal with structures that survive after a disaster. The EPA will go home by home to certify that a structure is fit for human occupancy after a water disaster such as a hurricane or flooding. Another area for federal regulation on mold is when a federally funded mortgage is being issued on the property. In the inspection prior to the mortgage, the inspector will look for mold. A seller will be required to clean up the mold before such a mortgage is issued.

On the state law side, some states require full disclosure of all defects by the seller to the buyer, including the presence of mold. Many home/ lender inspectors will not clear a property unless it is mold-free. Again, your local laws may include more restrictions.

The EPA website offers two publications that are good to read if you have questions about mold and how to get rid of it. The first one is mostly directed at a residence: "A Brief Guide to Mold, Moisture, and Your Home." The second one, "Mold Remediation in Schools and Commercial Buildings," covers both residences and commercial buildings. It is directed at a building manager, custodian, or other person responsible for commercial buildings and school maintenance (such as a landlord).

The EPA website also offers instructions for removal of mold and video courses.

Other Information on Residential Hazards

✪   Office of Healthy Homes and Lead Hazard Control—U.S. Department of Housing and Urban Development (HUD)

LINK: www.hud.gov/offices/lead/

✪   Indoor Air Quality and State Radon Office Locator—U.S. Environmental Protection Agency (EPA)

LINK: www.epa.gov/iaq/contacts.html

✪   Mold Dangers and Resources—U.S. Environmental Protection Agency (EPA)

LINK: www.epa.gov/mold/moldresources.html

Finding the Law

This chapter helps the non-lawyer locate the law. One of the most frustrating things about being a landlord is that you are expected to follow local, state and federal laws, but no one ever tells you where these laws are. Welcome to the world of a lawyer. There is no one perfect place where all the laws are located, especially when you are looking for the laws of a small town. Much of what a lawyer does is track down the applicable laws and then apply them to the situation at hand. This is a brief introduction to that process.

LOCATING THE LAW

The most significant laws to any landlord are those of the state, county, and city where the rental property is located. While the landlord must follow both federal and state laws, the majority of states incorporate the federal statutes for major issues such as discrimination into their own statutes, with additions or extra requirements for the landlord.

Most states have anti-discrimination laws and state agencies that prosecute violators of those laws. As for laws about the number of occupants of a rental property or the specifics needed in the rental property structure, the landlord needs to look at local (city, town, county) laws.

Internet   The best place to find any law is on the Internet. In Appendix B we provide links to a number of legal sites that can assist the landlord in finding a particular law or regulation. For any federal housing questions, the best place to begin a search is at www.hud.gov, the site for the Department of Housing and Urban Development. The HUD site consistently provides accurate and up-to-date information, including links to other important websites. There are many other sites that are directed at generally increasing the public's knowledge of the law and legal documents. Many bar associations provide helpful information and links to other information sites.

For state laws, you can also begin with the Internet. In Appendix A we provide state-specific Internet sites for every state. We also include sites that are created by the state to disseminate information to both landlords and tenants.

As for local (city, town, township, county) laws, the particular local area may have a website. As cities are becoming Internet savvy, they are creating their own web pages that include the local laws. Check to see if your local city or county has a website. In addition, you may want to contact city hall or the local city building department to see if they have a brochure or written information on landlord/tenant laws. Some big cities have both a website and a department that provides the entire landlord/tenant code to anyone who asks.

Libraries   Even in our computer-oriented society, laws and legal help are still printed in books. Many local libraries have the current state statutes in printed format. Your local library will probably have a copy of your city/town's laws; if they do not you can usually obtain a copy from your city hall. Because your property must adhere to the local laws, it is imperative that you review your local laws. Your city/town laws may not be easy to read. Many times the laws that affect landlords are not in a neat section called landlord/tenant law. Most commonly these important laws are found in sections such as "public housing," "land use," "zoning," "building codes," or "residential housing." The administrative personnel who work in your city/town hall can be helpful in directing you to the area of law you need to look at, and consulting them would be a good place to start.

There are also law libraries that the public can use, especially for reviewing the federal and state laws. These law libraries are located in law schools and at the majority of Circuit Court buildings. Librarians, especially those in law libraries, are usually extremely helpful to the public. In addition to the actual printed laws there are books that will assist you in understanding the laws. Of course, most libraries now have public computers so you can also review the websites that we have listed.

Local Laws/ Association Rules

If your property is in a small town or a place that has not gotten around to setting up a website you will need to do some legwork to find the local rules that apply to renting. Start with your city hall. You may be able to get a copy of the particular laws or codes that directly affect the rental property. The people at city halls are usually very helpful to residents.

If your property is in a gated community, part of a condominium association, part of a cooperative association, or part of a homeowners association, do not forget to get a copy of the association's rules and policies. These have the effect of law on your property. You should have been provided with a copy of the rules when you made your purchase, or you can get a copy from the association's main office.

INTERPRETING LAWS

A word of warning here: anyone can get a copy of the law. With the vast resources of the Internet, anyone can download all current laws and even bills pending in Congress. However, that is not the whole story on staying out of trouble by following the law.

As any attorney will tell you, many laws are written by people who do not seem to speak a common form of English. Terms are vague; rules are couched in terms of *maybe* and *could be*. Reading the actual law can be an exercise in confusion, especially when you are just looking for a simple answer to a simple question.

Furthermore, the law is interpreted by courts on a daily basis. So a law that says you must do a certain thing to rent out your property can be interpreted by judges to mean that doing that certain thing really means the landlord must do that one thing plus five other things. It is confusing. In order to really know what is going on with the law, an attorney must know what the law says, what the makers of the law really meant, and the latest interpretation of the law by the courts.

You may decide it is much easier to find an attorney who concentrates on handling landlord/tenant law than to try to find and interpret those laws on your own.

When You Are Accused of Violating the Law

Being accused of violating the law is one of the worst things that can happen in any person's life. It does not matter if you are completely innocent or just made an innocent mistake, being accused in a court or a hearing is an awful experience. It is also a time when you need expert help. That expert help comes from your attorney.

DEALING WITH LOCAL ZONING VIOLATIONS, BUILDING CODE VIOLATIONS, AND VARIANCES

You are going along as a landlord, handling tenants, getting rent, doing the right thing. Then all at once you get a notice from your city or town that your property is in violation of some zoning ordinance, building code, or a variance. This is usually an issue regarding the structure of the building, a repair not made in accordance with the law, or an encroachment by the property.

The first step is not to ignore the citation. Yes, in many cases it looks like a parking ticket, but this is not something that can be shoved in the glove box and ignored. You need to get information on what is wrong and how can it be fixed. In many towns this is as simple as calling the Building and Codes department (the department that issued the citation) and asking to talk to the inspector who wrote the citation. Respectfully ask for information on the problem, what fix is proper, and how long you have to make the repair. This is not the time to be belligerent with the city employee; the employee is just doing his or her job.

If the issue is not simple or you believe that the city is wrong, you may need to appeal. This will probably bring you into a hearing in front of a city council or board. Let me urge you, if you find yourself in this position, not to represent yourself. Do yourself a favor and hire an attorney to get you through this. Boards and city councils are actually legal bodies run similarly to a regular courtroom. There are procedures and an order in which the evidence must be presented. There are also rules about what evidence can be presented and when witnesses are allowed. While these boards and councils may look innocuous, they can cause you much expense and many problems if not approached in the proper manner. If you hire an attorney who has experience in these types of violations, you may be able to resolve the issue with minimal expense.

DEALING WITH A FEDERAL DISCRIMINATION COMPLAINT OR A CIVIL RIGHTS COMPLAINT

Any landlord can find themselves the subject of a discrimination complaint filed by a tenant or potential tenant with a state or federal agency. The landlord's response to this type of complaint determines whether the issue will be handled at the agency level or will proceed to a potentially expensive court proceeding. Understand that any of these agencies have the power to cost the landlord a large sum of money, even though they are not a traditional court.

Each agency has the power to levy fines on the landlord or issue a court order called an injunction that forces the landlord to either do something (for example: rent to a particular person) or stop doing something (for example: stop an eviction and reimburse the person filing the complaint for his or her attorney's fees and other expenses). Some state and federal agencies can levy fines for punitive damages, a costly amount that is meant to punish a person for a wrongdoing. What the agencies cannot do is have you arrested or put you in jail. To be arrested a person must commit a criminal act. To be sentenced to jail a person must be found guilty in a court of law.

If you receive such a complaint you must not ignore the documents or refuse to cooperate under the sad notion that the agency will not pursue you, because it will. Procedurally, once a complaint is filed with an agency an independent investigator will be assigned to investigate the complaint. The investigators really are independent and unbiased. Landlords who refuse to cooperate or even be civil to an investigator because "they are on the tenant's side" set themselves up for failure by losing the opportunity to plead their case to the investigator.

The more effective response is to cooperate fully with the investigator, provide all the documents requested, respond to all questions on time, and show how eager you are to resolve the complaint. If you believe there was no violation, present copies of all the evidence you have to the investigator. Work with the investigator to find out why the tenant filed the complaint and how the complaint can be resolved without further litigation. If you know that what was done was in violation of a rule, admit your mistake, offer to make amends to the person who filed the complaint, and make changes to ensure the mistake will not happen again.

The worst thing that a landlord can do when receiving one of these complaints is to be purposefully belligerent to the investigator and stonewall the investigation. For the landlord's financial health, the goal should be to resolve the complaint as quickly as possible before the complaint turns into a federal case. In instances such as these, the assistance and advice of an attorney can be invaluable.

It is common for a potential tenant to accuse a landlord of not renting to him or her due to discrimination. That is why the tenant-screening process that we present in this book, which uses the same criteria for all prospective tenants and uses the same forms for all prospective tenants, is so important. When a landlord is accused of not renting to a person due to discrimination, the landlord then shows the investigator his or her procedures, the forms used, and the records kept.

SECTION 4

THE LEASE

This section is all about the most important document that a landlord will use, the lease. We examine types of leases and important lease clauses, and discuss how to get the document signed.

Creating a Workable Lease

Agreements between landlords and tenants are usually expressed in terms of a lease. A lease is a written document signed by both the landlord and the tenant that describes the terms of the rental. However, that is not the end of what a lease can or cannot do for the landlord.

PREPARING LEASES AND RENTAL AGREEMENTS

A rental lease is a contract between two parties that details the rental of a piece of property, whether it is an apartment, a house, a garage, a parking spot, or a piece of land. The owner of the property agrees to let the renter of the property use the property under specific terms and conditions that are listed in the lease for a specified length of time.

Because the lease is a legal document it must adhere to the law regarding contracts, as well as federal, state, and local laws regarding rentals. This means the landlord cannot write a contract that absolves the landlord of liability for mistakes or errors, putting the financial burden on the tenant. The lease contract cannot be based on fraud, deception, false promises, misrepresentation of a material fact, or the concealment of a material fact.

The lease must adhere to the laws regarding discrimination by race, color, religion, nation of origin, families with children, pregnancies, disabilities, and sex. The lease must also include any clauses that are required by state, county, and local law. (See Appendix A.)

TYPES OF LEASES

There are four major types of leases that are used by landlords; your state may provide other options.

Agreement to Lease   This type of contract is frequently used in commercial leases and when a rental building is in the process of being built. Many of these in-progress buildings, in order to open up at the completion of the building phase with full occupancy, will pre-rent the units. This is not an application that a tenant fills out in the tenant screening phase, and legally this document does not create a landlord/tenant relationship; it is only a contractual agreement that a lease will be signed in the future. This type of contract should contain a penalty clause for the tenant who changes his or her mind about renting. In most cases a hefty security deposit or deposit to hold the rental will be required when signing this agreement.

The average landlord may want to use this type of contract in cases when your building is being renovated. Another place to use this document is if your rental building is a great seller and you have people who want to be put on a waiting list for the next opening. An agreement to lease can indicate how serious a potential tenant is about your rental property.

Rental Contract   A rental contract contains the same provisions and clauses as a standard lease except there is no actual date stating when the agreement will end. This type of lease is used for what are referred to as open-ended tenancies or month-to-month tenancies. The contract protects the landlord during the month the tenant is living in the rental property and provides the landlord with the legal backing for eviction if the tenant refuses to pay or leave the premises.

Many residential motels, which are motels for those temporarily transferred into an area or who are looking for a home in an area, use this type of lease. For many of the major hotel chains who offer this service, the contract is a very simple half-page form requiring the renter's name, home address, social security number, a credit card/bank account number to be charged, and a signature agreeing to the charge.

Rental with an Option to Buy

This lease is basically the standard lease agreement with the addition of a legal section that designates the terms for the potential purchase. These terms include: how much of the monthly rent is put toward a down payment for purchasing the property; what happens to that money during the term of the lease; who gets the interest on money that is banked; how the money is held at the bank (whether the money is in one party's account or in escrow); how long this agreement with the option continues; how both sides can cancel the option to buy; what happens if the property is destroyed; what happens if the property goes into foreclosure; and many other clauses which in extreme detail map out the complex agreement of renting with an option.

This type of agreement was very popular decades ago, before the latest housing market increases. It went out of favor when mortgage money was available to all, no matter their income or if they even had a down payment. Now, it may be coming back into fashion. In May of 2009 a Chicago newspaper heralded "A New Way to Buy a Home—Rent with an Option." Obviously these agreements are not new, but they are gaining new interest. They allow potential buyers to rent a home for a monthly amount plus an additional amount that goes toward a down payment. The rules of the standard landlord/tenant agreement still apply. The only difference is that the landlord has the additional accounting phase of taking the tenant's money and putting it toward a down payment.

This type of agreement can be tricky and should be drafted by professionals who are experienced in this type of transaction. Your real estate professional may be able to handle most of this deal and may even be able to match the property with clients who want a rent with an option.

Residential Rental Lease or Rental Lease or Standard Lease or Fixed-Term Lease

The residential rental lease is commonly known as the lease to rent. It is an agreement between the landlord and the tenant that starts the landlord/tenant relationship. It is usually written for a minimum period of one year. In this document the landlord must include all legally required information in addition to those clauses that will protect the landlord and the rental property. When people refer to a rental lease, this is the document most are talking about. The next chapter is devoted to this document.

Clauses in a Lease

This chapter concentrates on the individual clauses in a rental lease. We will be using some of the forms at the end of the book to explain the common clauses in a lease and those clauses that we have found are just good business. We will also discuss the reasons to use a lease and answer the question, "Will that preprinted lease from my stationary store work?"

CLAUSES IN A STANDARD LEASE

A rental lease agreement is built from independent clauses, or sections. The way that most leases are written is that each clause/section addresses only one subject, with like subjects are grouped together. For example, clauses about how much the rent is, when it is due, and the penalty for late rent are grouped together for ease of reading.

Each state has landlord/tenant rules that require that the lease contain certain elements or clauses. Actually every government agency that controls your rental property (state, county, city, town, township, etc.) can require that the lease agreement contain certain clauses. A landlord needs to check the local laws where the rental property is located to be sure his or her lease includes the required clauses.

While laws can require certain clauses, the majority of leases all include certain basic information. The following are the common clauses required in every state (refer to Form 05 001, p.279).

Basic Information

Name, Address, Contact Phone Number of Landlord

In most states there must be some method to contact a landlord. If the landlord has selected a property management company, that company's name and contract information will be there. The reason for this is in case of an emergency.

Name and Identification of All Tenants Who Are Signing the Lease

All legal tenants must provide some identification in order to sign the lease. Nicknames or aliases are not sufficient in most states. In the tenant application, you may want include the address of the tenant's nearest relative. If the tenant abandons the property while still owing rent, the landlord will need this information.

Address/Description of the Rental Property

A lease is a legal document, and it requires certain specificity about exactly what is being rented. For example: "Unit 3A at 4324 Warrenville Road, Chicago, Illinois, plus access to the common areas included at 4324 Warrenville Road, a ten-story apartment building," or "The single family home at 1440 Austin Boulevard, Chicago, Illinois, including the unattached two-car garage and yard."

Starting Date of the Lease

This is the actual date the tenancy begins.

Term of Lease

This is how long this lease lasts (one year, two years, etc.). It is also good to include the actual date that the lease will expire.

Rent and Limitations

The Amount of Rent Charged

This is the exact dollar amount of rent due each period (usually a month).

How the Rent is Paid and the Form the Rent Can Take

There can be no question as to the procedure of how the rent is paid and what form that rent will take. For example: "Payment by check made out to Erwin Property LLC, dropped off at complex office." Whatever procedure you decide to use, the lease must be clear on how the tenant is to pay to rent and the form of rent payment that is acceptable (usually a check).

When Rent Is to Be Paid

As part of the rent section you must put in when the rent is due. For example: "Rent is due the first of every month and will be deemed as late after the fifteenth of the month."

The full rent section should resemble this sample: "Rent is $750 per month, which is due on the first of every month. Rent should be paid in the form of a personal check made out to Mr. John Jones, and mailed to Mr. John Jones, 123 Briar Ave., Melrose Park, Illinois 60605. Rent should be mailed so that it arrives at the Melrose Park address by the first of the month. Rent arriving after the fifteenth of the month will be considered late and subject to any penalties listed in this lease."

Security of Damage Deposit Information

Many communities require that certain security deposit information be listed in the lease. For more information, see the chapter on security deposits.

Limitations on Property Use (Residential Cannot Be Commercial)

There are usually certain limitations on property use that must be included in a rental lease. For an association, the landlord would want to reference the rules of the property, such as, "The tenant must follow the rules provided in the document, Rules of 14440 Warrenville Road." Some rentals do not include a garage or parking space unless the tenant pays more, and that limitation would be stated here. Also, many people who are renting out their homes are not including barns, sheds, or other outbuildings on the land because they are storing family items there. If your rental includes any limitation on property use, it must be included in writing.

Limitations on the Number of People Living in Premises (in Accordance with Local Law)

You probably should include a limitation on the number of people who may live in the rental. You may also want to include a clause that requires anyone staying on the premises longer than two weeks be included on the lease.

Other Requirements per Local Law

If state or local law requires you to include other provisions in the lease, you must do so. Using the same language as the state/local requirement will make it easy to prove your compliance, should you ever be challenged.

*   *   *   *   *

Whew! Yes, that is a lot of information that must be captured on just a basic lease. And there is more. For a rental lease to accurately handle your rented property, you will need to include even more clauses to address each and every potential issue. The following are some suggested clauses that seasoned landlords use for their property. While using all the basic and suggested clauses is great, your property may still need additional protections. Those are up to you to draft into your lease or to have your attorney include in your lease. If you are in an area where the local government requires many, many clauses in a lease (like Chicago), your lease must include your needs plus those legally required clauses.

Suggested Clauses

Maintenance Clause

Your lease should state who is responsible for what maintenance. You may want your tenant to be responsible for mowing the lawn, shoveling the snow on the sidewalk, and numerous other tasks. These tasks should all be listed in this clause.

Limitations of the Landlord's Liability within the Law

A landlord cannot put something into a lease that will absolve him or her of legally required duties. For example the landlord cannot say, "If the apartment has no heat it is not my fault."

Insurance

You may want a requirement in the lease that the tenant must obtain rental insurance that will, at minimum, cover losses to the landlord caused by the tenant's negligence.

Limitations on Subletting, Adding Cotenants, or Assignment of the Lease by the Tenant

This clause allows the landlord to control who is living in the property. It also is a way to make sure that anyone who lives in the property is responsible for the rent.

Abandonment

The lease should state what is considered abandonment, and what the landlord's options are when the tenant abandons the rental premises.

Late Fees and Penalties for Bounced Rent Checks or Late Monthly Rental Payments

The lease should include a specific dollar amount charge that will be assessed to the tenant for late rent, and late rent should be defined. For example: "Rent will be considered late if not received by the landlord by the fifteenth of the month in which it is due." There should also be a specific dollar penalty imposed for rent checks that do not clear the bank. This penalty should include the bank fee charged to the landlord for a Not Sufficient Funds check plus an extra amount to cover any other fee.

Locks

The lease should forbid tenants to change the locks without the landlord's permission. This allows the landlord continuous access to his or her property even during the tenancy. This provision may be required by law in certain cities.

Limitations on Parking of Cars or Other Recreational Vehicles

The lease may require that license plates of tenants' cars be registered, that all vehicles have current state/city tags, that vehicles must be drivable, and that vehicles deemed abandoned (without current tags) will be towed at the owner's expense. This prevents the landlord's property from becoming a dumping ground for junk cars.

Area Designated for Tenant's Storage

Most multi-unit buildings have a place for the tenant to store items that do not fit in the rental unit. The storage area is usually a fenced in or gated area for each individual tenant, which is locked. If there is such an area, the lease should state where it is.

Who Pays Utilities and Other Fees

The lease should be specific as to who is responsible for connecting and paying for utilities. Often the tenant must contact the utility to get service in his or her name.

Landlord's Approval of Any Alterations or Improvements on the Rental Property

This clause should at least require that the tenant contact the landlord before making any permanent changes to the property. The landlord may also want to include language regarding any changes made without approval. The landlord can require that any alteration be restored back to original state at the cost of the tenant.

What Happens to the Tenant's Property Left After Eviction or After the Tenant Moves

It is not unusual for a tenant to leave a rental without notice, leaving some of his or her property behind. The landlord should include a clause in the lease that after a period of time the tenant's abandoned property will be disposed of. Check your local laws on this; some cities require that the property be held for a period of time, usually thirty days, before disposal.

How Deductions for Property Damage Are Calculated and Taken from the Security Deposit

This clause spells out the procedure that the landlord uses for calculating security deposit deductions. It can often be the directly copied from the local law. We discuss security deposits in a later chapter.

Landlord's Access to Rental Premises

This clause lists times when a landlord can enter the rental property without the tenant's permission, and delineates how much notice the landlord must give prior to a scheduled access. This clause must comply with the local law.

Tenant's Use of Other Facilities on the Property

In this clause the landlord should list the other parts of the property that the tenant may use, such as common areas, a storage locker, the laundry room, the garage, etc.

What Happens at the End of the Lease

In this clause the landlord needs to be both specific and within the local law. Is the tenancy automatically renewed? Does the tenant get a notice that he or she is not being renewed? What happens when the tenant does not move out at the end of the lease?

Making the Rental Property a No-Smoking Area

It is becoming more and more common for rental properties to be designated no-smoking buildings. This is especially true with those who are renting out their family home. Make sure that the prospective tenant knows about this before he or she agrees to rent from you. You may also want to penalize the tenant if you find that he or she has smoked in the property. The most common penalty is that the tenant pays for a full cleaning of the property.

The Effect on the Tenant of a Sale of or Foreclosure on the Building

It is common for a rental lease to state that if the building is sold, the rental agreement remains in force and continues with the new owner.

The issue of foreclosure, however, is a new inclusion into rental agreements since all property owners, even landlords, are subject to losing their property to foreclosure. It is up to the landlord whether to put in language about foreclosure. A common clause on foreclosure is that the landlord will provide the tenant with some notice and will follow the local laws regarding the keeping of security deposits. Obviously if the landlord is going to attempt to apply the security deposits to the mortgage, it would be very foolish to state otherwise.

What the Landlord Does When the Tenant Defaults on the Lease

Commonly the landlord merely asserts his or her ability under the law to evict a tenant who defaults on the lease.

Reference to and Incorporation of the Landlord's Written Rules for Tenants

Reference to and Incorporation of the Landlord's Written Rules on Companion Animals

A Statement that this Property and the Landlord follow the Laws of the City, County, State, and All Applicable Federal Laws in the Renting of the Premises

WHERE TO GET A LEASE

A landlord can effectively write his or her own lease. See form 05 001, p.279, for an example. However, the landlord must make sure that all local and federal laws are followed in this document. Because the lease is the legal basis of the entire landlord/tenant relationship it is important that the lease document contain the maximum amount of protection for the landlord and the property that the law will allow. As such, this may not be the time for the landlord to create his or her own legal document.

A landlord may be able to find a sample lease or prepared leases that are used in the rental area from real estate professionals, local rental organizations, or from those organizations that assist landlords. Many of these organizations can be found on the Internet.

Finally, the landlord can have his or her attorney draft a lease that will not only include everything that the landlord wants but will adhere to all laws. This way the landlord can have the agreement tailored to what is important to him or her. This is especially important if you are going to enter into a lease with an option to buy agreement. Of course, the best thing a landlord can do is to have his or her attorney draft a lease that fits everything the landlord wants plus local and federal laws.

DO YOU NEED A WRITTEN LEASE?

The question always comes up: does a landlord really need a written lease? It is a hassle to create one and may cost a bunch to have an attorney draft one. Still, the answer is a resounding *yes*. A landlord needs a written lease for the protection of the rental property.

Furthermore, the Statute of Frauds requires that any agreement for real property, such as a lease, that extends beyond one year must be in writing. That is the law in all states. Even if you are renting your property for less than a year, you still need a written lease.

A lease is a list of legal obligations on both sides, but especially on the tenant. This agreement lists the amount of rent, who pays for what maintenance, and other financial aspects. It also lists or incorporates rules that can cause the landlord to evict the tenant. Finally a lease provides for the landlord a means of reimbursement from the tenant who breaks a lease, who damages the property, or who does any of the numerous things tenants do that cost the landlord money. Without a written agreement any court fight between the landlord and tenant becomes a he said/she said fight. You must arm yourself with a tool to win that fight, and that tool is a written lease agreement.

LOCAL LAW

Most states have requirements for what can and cannot be included in a rental lease. It is of utmost importance that the landlord be aware of these laws. In some states violating the law about what can be included in a lease can jeopardize the entire lease contract.

For example, in the beginning of 2008 the state of Alabama passed a law that made four lease clauses unenforceable in existing leases and prohibited them in new leases. The four clauses arc: 1) A tenant cannot waive his or her rights that are given under the law; 2) A lease cannot contain a confession of judgment due to nonpayment of rent, meaning the landlord must go through a court proceeding to get a judgment against the tenant, even if the tenant does not pay the rent; 3) The landlord cannot force the tenant to pay the landlord's attorney's fees in cases of collections or evictions; and 4) The landlord cannot limit his or her liability.

If you have problems finding out what the law means in your state, look at the websites for tenants' rights in your state. (See Appendix A.) Many times websites addressed to the tenants have information about the law in a simpler, easier to read format.

Signing and Altering the Lease

This chapter discusses a very important part of any legal transaction—the procedure. Yes, we lawyers take our procedures very seriously. In some legal issues the procedures may be mandated by law to make the transaction legal. For the most part the procedures help us ensure that every required step or document is handled in the correct manner.

SIGNING THE LEASE

The lease should list and require the signatures of all tenants and co-tenants who are renting the premises, and the landlord. Some states require witnesses and a notary to approve the signatures, but most do not. The issue of cotenants is one area where landlords tend to be lax and tenants may take advantage of the landlord's inattention.

GOLDEN RULE: Everyone who is going to be living in the rental premises *must* go through the same screening (credit check, employment check, etc.). Everyone who is going to be living in the rental premises *must* sign the lease.

Tenants must repeatedly be told that each one who signs the lease is liable for the rent. If one person leaves the rental, too bad, the rent is still due in full. Each tenant is legally agreeing to pay the entire rent, even if his or her buddy or significant other leaves. Everyone who is living in the rental must sign.

A landlord can check to see who is living in his or her rental by watching who is receiving mail at that address, who is seen at the address, and who is there when the landlord stops by for a visit.

Most communities limit the number of people living in any rental unit. This is especially true in apartment complexes and in condominiums. That maximum number should be part of the lease, as should the agreement by the tenants not to take on additional cotenants without permission of the landlord.

When tenants do decide to add valid cotenants, or to sublease, or in any manner to change who is living in the rental property, the landlord *must* require that the new tenants be screened and sign a lease. Only by consistent screening and by requiring all tenants to sign a lease can the landlord protect the rental property.

SIGNING THE LEASE (FORM 05 001)

The actual signing of the lease is usually very simple, but check with your state law to see if a notary is required to be present at the signing. All those who are listed as tenants must sign the lease document.

This is a common procedure for signing the lease:

- ✪   The landlord hands the tenant(s) two copies of the lease document. Both the landlord's copy and the tenant's copy will be signed by both parties.

- ✪   The landlord will go over certain facts as stated on the lease. Is the name of each tenant spelled correctly? Are the names of all tenants listed on the lease? Are those people present for the signing? Is there anyone else who will be living in the rental property? Are there any questions on the lease?

✪ The landlord may ask if each tenant understands the amount of rent, that rent is due on the (first) of every month, where to park, the amount of security deposit required, and other important rules. Most landlords do this just to remind the tenant about the most serious rules that must be followed.

✪ The landlord will explain that the security deposit is not the last month's rent, and how damages are determined.

✪ The landlord should then ask for the first month's rent and the security deposit and then issue the tenant two receipts for this money.

✪ Both landlord and tenant should then sign both lease documents (one for the landlord and one for the tenant).

✪ Any other documents, such as a companion animal agreement (form 09 002, p.286) or garage rental, should be handled at this point.

Once all documents are signed the landlord should make sure that both parties (the landlord and the tenant) have copies of all signed documents. The landlord may want to provide the tenant with a copy of the rules for the rental property, if that has not already been done. The landlord should then hand the tenant the keys to the rental property.

CHANGING THE LEASE

Many times a landlord desperately needs to make changes in an existing lease. Perhaps the cost of heating or electricity has increased or the rental property is in need of some major, expensive renovations. What can be done at that point depends 1) on the local law; and 2) on how the original lease was structured. Only a few states allow clauses that let the landlord increase the rent during a contracted term, and even then it can be done only in some very restrictive cases. It is rare to be able to increase rent during the lease term. For this reason the landlord must be careful when setting the rent, because he or she will live with it for the term on the lease. This is also why tenants want to sign a lease, so that they can have some security that their rent will not increase.

In a mixed commercial and residential lease there may be a very limited increase for certain commercial items. Please contact a local attorney who is experienced in commercial rental law if you want to write potential changes into your commercial lease.

SECTION 5

THE RENTAL AMOUNT

This section is all about one of the major reasons we are landlords—the rent. This is our pay, the money that supports our family and keeps the rental property in good shape. Here we discuss three important concepts on the rental payment: how to calculate what rent to charge; how to collect the rent; and how specialized rent is calculated.

How to Calculate the Rental Payment

For most landlords the top question is: How much do I charge for rent? The general rule is that the amount charged as rent should cover all expenses and provide some cushion for unexpected events and profit. Most people underestimate the amount of their expenses, so be careful. Of course, you also want to keep the rent charge in line with what others charge for rent in your town.

SETTING THE RENT

Looking at the Expenses

If you are like most of us you list your expenses in your head at night and wonder how you will be able to pay for everything. It is one of those universal worries that the majority of U.S. citizens have in common. Now that you have decided to become a landlord, it is time to bring that list out of the dark recesses of the night.

You will need your receipt bag or box, a pad of paper, and a pen. You want to list all the expenses that are standard for the property that you are planning to rent. The best way is to look at the expenses for the past twelve months, keeping track of the expenses by month. Why? Because your major bills (gas, electric, house insurance) are usually either done per month or per year (so that you can divide the yearly payment by twelve). You are looking for those standard expenses such as:

○ gas;

○ electric;

○ water;

○ garbage pickup;

○ lawn maintenance;

○ heating oil;

○ home insurance;

○ taxes;

○ mortgage payment;

○ other loans on the home, and payments on things bought for the home such as a new furnace, air conditioner, windows, etc.; and

○ any other payment that you are making for this property.

What you should end up with is a list of what you pay on this property over a twelve-month period. Remember that large annual bills, like taxes, should be divided into twelve monthly payments. Now, add up the expense for each month. You should have a total that is very similar for each month. If you do not, concentrate on the larger number. This number is approximately what you should charge in monthly rent.

We say approximately because this number will need to be increased to match any increases in the costs of services such as utilities and to cover maintenance on the rental property. Plus as a landlord you may want to add an amount so that you not only cover all the expenses you have today, but those cost increases that will come up tomorrow and perhaps add just a bit of profit for yourself.

If you have a significant amount that you are paying in monthly mortgage, loans, and/or home equity bills you may not be able to cover these expenses in a fair rental amount. Remember, a fair rental amount is what a tenant will pay for rent in your area.

Eliminating Some Costs

Next you want to look at your expenses to see if there are some items that you are paying for now, but that once you get a tenant in, the tenant will pay for. The first thing that comes to mind is the telephone service. For a multi-unit building you may also have the tenants pay directly for their heating and/or electricity. Our seasoned landlords already have this decided, but for our new landlords, how do you decide what the tenant pays for?

Let's start by assuming that the tenant is responsible for his or her telephone service in your rental. So, when preparing your rental you will probably need to speak with the telephone company about your decision. It may be simpler for you to leave an actual telephone in the rental for the tenant's use once the tenant gets service hooked up.

Next we need to look at the other utilities and how they are hooked up. The utilities are electricity, gas, oil, and water. They may be referred to as heating and air conditioning. We know that in a single family home and even in some multiple-unit buildings the utilities can be installed as just one hookup (especially when the building has only one furnace/air conditioner) and there is only one bill. We also know that in multiple-unit buildings these same utilities can be hooked up in a separate manner where each unit has its own furnace/air conditioner/hot water heater and each unit is sent a separate bill.

So, using the information for your rental, it is up to you to decide what the tenant pays for. It is easy in a multi-unit building where the utility bills are already being sent to each unit to require that each tenant pay his or her own utility bills.

The hard part comes in situations where the bill comes to the landlord and has to be divided up between units, or, even worse, when the landlord is renting a single family home to one tenant. If you are renting out your family home because you cannot sell it right now do you really want to take the chance that your tenant will continue to pay the utility bills? Do you trust the tenant to pay the bills every time, on time, or will the tenant abandon the property in the dead of winter with no heat or water?

When calculating what needs to be included in the rental charge you will need to determine how the utilities are set and who is going to pay for them. Some landlords merely add an approximate amount for utilities to each tenant's rent and hope that this amount will cover the total bills. For many it is easier to approximate the utility charge than to take precious time each month calculating who needs to pay what. Remember, as a landlord your time is valuable.

Projecting Cost Increases

You will need to add a cushion in the rent for potential cost increases. We all know that costs will continue to rise. There is no question if they will rise, the question is how much. As a landlord you will need to estimate these increases and put that number in the rent. Since most leases are set up for a one-year duration and you will not be able to raise the rent, your guess better be accurate.

The costs we are speaking of here are utilities, insurance, taxes, and, if your mortgage/loan on the rental building has a provision that could make the payments increase, an amount for that. If you follow the business section of most newspapers you may be able to get a handle on utility increases. Tax increases may be estimated through your local government informational office.

Another thing to look at is what costs are covered by similar rentals in your neighborhood. The best place to find this information is in the rental section of your local newspaper. There you can see what other landlords are including, and even what they are charging as an average rental.

Adding a Cushion

One of the most common mistakes that landlords make when setting the rent is forgetting to put in a cushion. That cushion is not just for huge increases in costs that you did not see, it is for those unexpected events that are not covered by insurance. As landlord you are required to keep the rental property habitable. Heating units, water lines, and toilets are among those common things that do break and can make an entire building uninhabitable. So you will need to hold back some cushion for that future rainy day of problems.

In addition, as a landlord you need to get something out of this deal. So you should put in a cushion or a salary or a profit amount that pays you for your work.

SETTING THE RENTAL AMOUNT LOWER THAN EXPENSES

There are legitimate reasons for you to set the rent lower than the expenses you added up in the previous paragraphs. The biggest reason is that your property is sitting vacant, you have no offers for purchase, and you are now stuck paying two mortgages (one for the vacant house, and one for where you really live). The potential of foreclosure should be enough incentive. You need to be aware of what you will need to bring in from rent in order to keep this property out of foreclosure until you are able to sell it. For many, a rent payment that covers one half of the mortgage may be sufficient to avoid foreclosure.

The problem is that you and your vacant house are not alone. Many, many other people are sitting in the same exact situation. And they are trying to lure a tenant from the same limited number of potential renters. Therefore, when setting rent you need to keep your rental payment in the same range as comparable properties in your area. You may even want to be willing to discount the rental payment so when that perfect tenant comes in with stellar references and cash in hand you can say, "If you sign today I will discount the rent."

If you are working with your lender to refinance or to avoid foreclosure, a tenant who is willing to pay for most of the mortgage payment will be a great place to start negotiations. So, yes, it is reasonable to set the rental amount lower than your expenses and take a monthly loss on the property. Not only is it reasonable, it is happening all over the United States.

Do not get discouraged. The real estate market can be a boom for you no matter which way it is going. When mortgage money is hard to get, more people will want to rent. When mortgage money is easy to get, there will be more buyers for your property.

SETTING THE RENT WITH AN OPTION TO BUY

For many landlords who really want to sell the property there is another option. This option may be complex, but is a win-win for everyone. It is renting with an option to buy. In this type of agreement the landlord takes a small portion of each monthly rental payment and puts that amount into a bank account, which accumulates interest. At the end of a selected period (usually a few years), the tenant has accumulated a down payment and can then get financing to purchase the rental property.

This is an agreement that must be in writing, so you will need an attorney to help. Because the rental is for longer than a one-year period, the landlord usually will charge an increased rent after the first year. There must be terms in the contract regarding what happens if the tenant decides not to buy. In many cases the tenant gets only a portion of the amount saved, but that depends on your area and the common way of handling this there.

Some of the best reasons for this type of agreement are that the landlord can charge more, the landlord does not have to deal with annual leases, and if the tenant thinks he or she may purchase the property he or she will be very careful with it.

INCREASING THE RENT

It is common for new landlords to get that sinking feeling once they collect the first month's rent, because the total amount of the rent does not meet the expenses from the rental property. This is especially true if the rental property has an adjustable rate mortgage or a balloon payment which comes due. If the lease is a month-to-month and there are terms in the lease that allow rent increases, the landlord merely notifies the tenant that next month the rent is increasing. For the more common yearly or fixed-term lease raising rent is more difficult.

The primary thing a landlord can do is to be totally sure of all current rent expenses as well as expenses that are scheduled to happen in the future (like the mortgage adjustment or balloon payment), and then add some cushion when calculating the rental rate. Yes, this is tough because in some cases the expenses for the rental exceed the amount that a landlord can get for rent. If that is your case, then you need to decide if you want to rent the property for less than what you are paying out or hold out for a tenant who is willing to pay a higher rent. Either way you are stuck paying the same expenses month after month. It would seem that even a tenant paying half those expenses would be better than nothing.

Most yearly leases do not allow for increases. That is the reason the tenant signs a one-year contract—for that one year the rent remains the same. Some states allow the landlord to insert a clause that allows for rent increases during the lease term, but these are for only special circumstances. A landlord will need to contact a local professional before including this complex lease clause. In most other cases, the landlord must wait until the lease term is over or the tenant is gone before raising the rent.

Collection of Rent

Determining what to charge for rent and putting that in writing is worthless unless the landlord sets up procedures for actually collecting the rent. This chapter talks about this aspect of being a landlord.

RULES ON THE COLLECTION OF RENT

For a landlord, there is one opportunity to make all the rules about getting the rental payment collected, and that opportunity is in crafting the lease document. This is something that you can tailor to what is convenient to you. Once you determine the rules you will need to put them in writing. The lease should contain these rules or at least reference a collection of rent rules that are printed on a separate form. All tenants should get a copy of the rules when they begin the rental and for each subsequent renewal.

Amount
It seems simple, but many leases forget to include this one crucial point—how much rent the tenant should pay.

When the Rent Is Due

The standard is that the rent is due on the first of the month. This is normal for both month-to-month rentals and for those leases that last a year or more.

When Rent Is Considered Late

The majority of residential and commercial leases specify a point when the rent will be considered late, the penalty for late rent, and how many late rents are allowed before the landlord initiates eviction proceedings. The time period used depends on your area. In many big cities the tenant has less than a week before the rent is considered late and an eviction complaint is filed with the local court.

Penalties for Late Rent

It is common to add on a fee for late rent. To keep the chronic late payers in check, a landlord should consider an increasing fee each time the rent is late during the term of the lease. Or the landlord may want to make the late fee a significant amount even for the first offense. Either way the landlord should be flexible enough to override the fee in the rare cases when the tenant has a legitimate emergency.

Currency

If the landlord or property manager is on the rental premises, the landlord may decide to accept cash rental payment. That is always tricky because the rental office should not be known as a place that keeps large amounts of cash. A landlord who has only a few rentals may even want to personally pick up the rent, but again there are concerns with people knowing that this person carries cash rental proceeds.

The other option is rental payment by check. Again, if the landlord is on the premises or likes a monthly personal visit, the check can be handed directly to the landlord. The landlord should then issue a simple receipt with the check number, amount, and date on the receipt. Inexpensive receipt books are available at office supply stores, general stores, and full service drugstores.

If the landlord lives off premises or if a property management company handles collection of the rent, the check will need to go into the U.S. mail. This can cause delays that the landlord needs to adjust to. An adjustment can be that the tenant is given several extra days for transport before the rent is considered late. The landlord may consider getting a post office box close to the rental property on the theory that the rental check has a shorter distance to travel. If the landlord does visit the building, he or she may want to install a lockbox in the building where tenants can deposit rent checks. Finally, the landlord can just tell the tenants about local slow mail service and insist that the tenant mail the rent check in plenty of time for delivery—just like the credit card companies do.

A rental check should be immediately deposited in the landlord's account and not drawn on until the landlord is sure that the check has cleared. That way any bounced checks will not endanger the landlord's credit.

Penalty for Bounced Checks

The lease must contain information about the penalty for bounced rent checks. This is a serious issue since most banks charge high fees for processing these checks. The penalty charged to the tenant must be sufficient to cover the costs that the landlord's bank charges plus the extra time that the landlord spends processing the check. Again, it is important that the landlord deposit the rental checks in his or her account and not draw on that account until all rental checks have cleared. In addition to a penalty for bounced checks, the landlord should require that after two bounced rental checks all rent must be paid by a cashier's check or a postal money order.

WHEN YOU HAVE A PROPERTY MANAGER

If you have hired a property management company they may already have set rules regarding how the rent is collected. Many property management companies have a lockbox system where checks are dropped off. Once a check arrives at the lockbox it is recorded and deposited. The landlord may be able to obtain information about payments online within a short period of time. Your property management company may have set rules on penalties for late payments, penalties for bounced checks, and how a lack of payment leads to eviction, and those rules should be included in the written lease.

If your property manager is an individual or has an office on the premises you will need to set up a procedure as to how the rent is collected, when it is deposited, and what records should be made of the transaction. These procedures need to allow you to capture all the information you need to keep up with your accounting books, to make sure that the funds are secure, and to maintain a record of when tenants pay. An experienced property manager may be able to assist you with these procedures. Your bank's hours for deposits, your availability, and even the time it takes for a check to clear are some of things that may influence procedures for rent collection.

MINIMUM PROCEDURES TO FOLLOW

When setting up a method to collect rent the easiest step is to tell all tenants that they must bring a check for the rent to the office on the first of every month. The office may have a deposit/mail slot for after-hours drop-offs. When the check is dropped off, the office staff should provide the tenant with a written receipt noting the check number, the amount paid, the property the payment is for, the date paid, and the name of payer.

The rest is up to you. Many landlords will then enter this information into a paper accounting log, into a computer spreadsheet, or into a program that handles accounting chores.

The next step is to prepare the money/check to go to the bank. If you are dealing with a few checks and multiple deposits it may be best to make a copy of the check, or the receipt for cash, prior to any deposits at the bank. These copies are then bundled with the receipt from the bank. You can then take your time in posting this to a paper ledger or accounting software. Having that paper copy of the actual check can also help if there is a glitch at the bank or if one of the checks is mislaid. Once the deposit is made these copies can be clipped to the deposit receipt for further accounting work.

The landlord should require that all rent is deposited before the end of the business day in which it is received. For those times when there are many rental checks coming in, like the first day of each month, the landlord may want to require two deposits a day.

The key for any procedure that a landlord wants to use is control, even if the landlord is the only person on staff. As a landlord you will need to keep track of the amount paid in rent, the date it was paid, the person who paid it, the check number of the payment, the date it was deposited, and the date the bank clears the check. If you have staff or employees doing this for you, you must ensure that the money is handled in the same way each and every time. The same is true if you are doing it yourself. The majority of business owners have been in the situation where they are tired and want to get home, so what does it matter if just this one time they do not make a copy of a check or do not fill out the deposit slip properly? Well, unfortunately, those are inevitably the times when problems happen.

New Bank Security   Please note: In the bank restructurings of 2009 many banks decided to implement a rule that those who are not authorized to sign on a particular account will not be provided with the total balance of that account, even when that person is making a deposit. For practical purposes this means that your employees who are not authorized to write a check on the corporate account may continue to make deposits, but they will no longer get a receipt that lists the balance amount in the account. The bank will only provide a non-signatory with a receipt noting the amount deposited and the date. This is to protect employers who routinely allow employees to deposit into the corporate bank accounts.

USING RENT COLLECTION TO CHECK ON YOUR PROPERTY

Many landlords, especially those who are renting out their family home for the first time, are understandably concerned with how the tenants are treating their property. These landlords may decide to collect the rent in person and, at the same time, take a look at how the tenants are taking care of the property. There is nothing at all wrong with this way of collecting rent; in fact, your tenant may welcome the friendship.

Many landlords do not have the time or the inclination to work in a personal visit every month, especially when both the tenant and landlord have other jobs to go to. If you can make that monthly visit, look around, be helpful, and enjoy telling your tenant about how important this home is to you too.

COLLECTING LATE RENT

We have a chapter on problems with tenants which goes into problems with late rent. Let's face it, as a landlord you will get involved in late rent at least once. Tenants have various reasons for not paying their rent on time. In today's economic climate that reason often is a loss of a job. What you do as a landlord in this case is up to you, local laws, and your own financial well-being.

Even good tenants can run into money problems. Before that happens you should become aware of your options as landlord. You should have a penalty clause in your lease that will provide you with some extra money from those who are late in the rent payment. You should also include in your lease a clause about how many times a tenant can be late without you initiating an eviction. In addition, you may want a clause that allows you to not renew the lease and/or to break the lease if the tenant repeatedly pays the rent late. Remember, these clauses are not cast in stone. You can override any clause in the lease, but it is important that these penalties are in place in your lease for times when you do want to evict a problem tenant.

Even if a landlord can legally evict a tenant, the landlord may decide to try another route rather than undergo the legal expense of an eviction. Some landlords have allowed their very good tenants to work on the rental property in lieu of a certain portion of rent. The landlord may also waive the penalties for late rent. I know of a landlord who actually helped a tenant get another job so the tenant could pay rent.

Other Types of Rent

We end this section with a brief overview of other types of rent. This is certainly not an extensive analysis of these types of rent. If you are interested in any of these, please look at your local laws to see how your community handles them. You can also find more information in an Internet search or on the websites that we list.

RENT CONTROL

Rent control is a term that is used to mean several different things depending on the situation and location. In some parts of the country rent control means that the rent cannot be raised beyond a certain amount. Depending on the type of rent control, the landlord can get a stipend from the city, a tax break for the amount of rent lost, or nothing.

Certain co-ops require that owners of the units keep within certain boundaries with the amount of rent charged for one of the units. This is done to keep the number of investors who just purchase a unit and then rent it out to a minimum. Co-ops really want all residents to be owners. Some condominium and gated community complexes are also adopting rules that limit the rentals, often by instituting rent controls or charging extra fees to owners who rent.

Another type of rent control occurs through programs in which the landlord receives money from the government for renting to low-income tenants. The most common program of this type is through the Department of Housing and Urban Development (HUD).

HUD   The Housing Choice Voucher Program, commonly called Section 8, provides tenant-based and project-based financial assistance from the federal government. It is operated by the Department of Housing and Urban Development (HUD) and gets its name because the law which covers this program is at Title 24, Chapter IX, Part 982—Section 8. The primary goal of this program is to provide low-income families, the elderly, and the disabled with the ability to obtain safe, decent, and affordable housing.

Landlords and property owners who provide Section 8 rental units are subject to an additional governing body, the Housing Authority. Some cities have a local HUD office, and that would be the landlord's direct contact. Housing authority rules require that the rental facilities be maintained in a decent, safe, and sanitary condition. The unit must pass the local program's housing standards and continue to be maintained at that level. HUD will also enforce the terms and services that are listed in the lease.

When renting to those with Section 8 vouchers the landlord is under an additional obligation to avoid discriminating against tenants because of race, religion, sex, age, sexual orientation, or disability. HUD provides tenants and potential tenants several methods to file discrimination complaints, including filling out a form on the Internet.

Before even looking for a rental unit, the potential tenant must apply to HUD for a rent voucher. HUD will determine if the person is eligible based on several factors such as income, assets, and number of people in the family. This information is verified and the person is investigated to make sure the information is accurate. Once the potential tenant qualifies for a rental voucher, his or her local HUD office may be able to provide a list of rental properties that accept the rental voucher, or the potential tenant may be on his or her own when searching for a rental unit. Once the potential tenant finds a possible rental unit, he or she views the unit and goes through the same screening that the landlord requires for other tenants.

HUD information for tenants consistently reminds them that a lease is a legal contract and that they must abide by the terms of the lease. Tenants must also follow local ordinances and the rules of the rental community. They must provide accurate information regarding their eligibility for the voucher. Section 8 tenants must also pay the correct amount of rent at the time specified by the lease.

HUD reminds tenants that they are responsible for keeping their rental unit clean, disposing of garbage properly, complying with local health and safety codes, and reporting any building defects to the landlord.

Federally assisted housing can financially benefit a landlord with loans and grants. Landlords who are interested need to contact their local Housing Authority, review their local ordinances to see if this is feasible, and review HUD information. However, any acceptance of government money comes with additional legal requirements. Most HUD information is online at **www.hud.gov**.

Low-Income Housing Other than HUD

Tenants with low incomes may be eligible for housing assistance other than Section 8 vouchers. Federal assistance is also available for:

✪ **Public Housing:** This is low-income housing that is operated by the local housing authority.

✪ **Privately Owned Subsidized Housing:** In this case the federal government provides a subsidy to the property owner. The owner then applies this money toward the rent payment for specific people under different programs. There are programs for the elderly, the disabled, low-income families, and low-income individuals. These programs are also operated by the local Housing Authority.

✪ **HUD's HOME Program:** This program provides grants to state and local governments to offer low-income housing.

✪ **Rural Housing Service:** The local Rural Development office operates this program, which is funded by the Department of Agriculture. It provides financial assistance and low-cost loans for those who qualify.

Your state may also have local programs administered through the local HUD office or through a state operated housing assistance center.

What all these programs have in common is that the rent is controlled for the tenants. The control is done by HUD or the housing authority that administers the program.

SECTION 6

PREPARING THE PROPERTY

This section covers getting your property ready to actually rent out. First we look at your family home as a rental. There are several changes that the family home should go through before the tenants walk through the door.

We then look at renting out your vacation home. Being the landlord for a vacation home has its own set of problems and benefits.

We then look at insurance on your rental property and what you need to know in order to protect your property with proper insurance.

Finally we talk about how to market your rental property—how to get that tenant who will care for your rental property as if it were his or her own.

Your Property

This chapter looks at your property from several different perspectives including your personal feelings, what should be left in the property, and common ways to get a rental property ready for a tenant.

YOUR PROPERTY AS A RENTAL

OK, admit it, you like the property you are planning to rent out. It could be that this was your home before a job transfer, a financial crisis, or the purchase of a new home. It may even be the home you were raised in. It reflects your style and the things you feel are of value, and you do not want anyone messing with it. Do either of the following statements sound like you?

"I love my home and you are just temporarily borrowing it!"

"I rented out a lovely furnished house where I had meticulously decorated each room. To my surprise the tenant complained about the color of the purple toilet seat. Yes, it was functional. Yes, it was purple. It matched the small flowers in the wallpaper and shower curtain and the trim on the towels. I was tempted to just remove the toilet seat and let them sit on the porcelain. Their lease was not renewed."

That was me a few years ago. We all feel that way about our property, even if we own a multi-unit building. These units do reflect our style, our colors, and our decorating. There is always some emotional attachment, so expect it. Allow yourself time to adjust to that building no longer being your home or your family's home. There is a certain sadness about seeing someone else living in a home that meant so much to you, but take heart in knowing that the building is going to provide you with income.

Also expect that you will second-guess yourself about the decision to rent. Remind yourself that something has brought you to the decision to rent out your property. Begin by looking at what drove you here. Were you unable to sell this property and now have mortgages on two homes? Are you overwhelmed by bills and want to get rent as a way to avoid foreclosure? Do you want to keep this property in the family, but cannot afford to have it sit empty? All of these are good reasons to consider renting the property.

Stop—Before You Start Preparing for Tenants

If this is a family home or place that has sentimental value to you, do not lift one finger to prepare the property for tenants until you go through each room and take pictures. For those of us who had to rent out our parents' home after they passed just to keep the property in our family, pictures of how it was are great memories.

PREPARING FOR TENANTS

The Law

It is vital that you make sure that you can rent out this property. Some cities and towns have laws that require certain items be added to rental property (such as smoke detectors on every floor). Know what your city requires.

If your rental property is part of a gated community, cooperative, or condo association, make very sure that you can rent it out. Some of these organizations have rules that range from prohibiting owners from having any tenants to requiring permission for tenants from the organization. Violating the rules of these organizations brings legal problems to the landlord. While you are looking at the restrictions enforced by these organizations, also look carefully at the annual fee you pay to them. While some groups allow tenants, they will raise the annual fee charged to the owner/landlord to a point where the rent must be increased just to cover that charge.

Deciding What Goes with the Property

There are three options for rentals: furnished, semi-furnished, and unfurnished. Each area of the country may have its own definition of these terms, but in general the definitions below are sufficient..

Unfurnished

Unfurnished is usually reserved for the yearly or annual rentals. This is the standard apartment or home where the tenant is expected to stay long-term. The tenant is expected to bring his or her own furnishings into the rental. Items that are built in such as cabinets, closets, refrigerators, stoves, dishwashers, garbage disposers, lighting fixtures, or anything anchored on the wall or floor may be included in an unfurnished rental.

This is the way that most of us think about rentals, nothing in it except for the kitchen appliances, sinks, and toilet. Depending on the landlord and building an unfurnished unit may not even include all appliances. Also, if your rental includes both living quarters and an area for a commercial business, there may be no appliances included. However, unless the rental has a shared bathroom even commercial unfurnished includes toilet and sink.

As landlord you can decide what unfurnished means to you and communicate that to your prospective tenants. You should also be aware of what unfurnished means in your area. In many parts of the country it is common for an unfurnished rental to come with a washer and dryer. Read the local rental ads to see what is common in your part of the country.

Semi-Furnished

Semi-furnished is totally vague term used when the landlord is supplying part but not all of the necessary furniture for the rental. This term is commonly used by landlords who do not want to be tied down to the requirements of renting a totally furnished place, but still want to leave some furniture in the unit. This happens a lot with the homeowner who has purchased a new home and cannot sell the one being rented. The homeowner may have duplicates of furniture or appliances and would prefer the extras just stay with the rental. Most tenants will appreciate anything left, but do not expect that these items will be in the same condition after a year or two of tenants.

As landlord you can decide what semi-furnished means to you, and make sure to use this in marketing to prospective tenants. Again, be aware of what other rental properties in your area are including. For many tenants, like those who rent for a short period of time like a school semester or a work project, the more the landlord can include in the property the better.

Furnished

Similar to a hotel, "furnished" can include everything, even maid service. The common understanding of furnished is that it includes towels, bed-linens, dinnerware, cooking utensils, a television, and all furniture. Many landlords have carved out a lucrative niche by renting furnished property to people who are in a city on temporary assignment or to students who only stay for the school year. Again, you must know your community and determine what will work in your area.

What is Left in the Rental Property? For landlords who are renting out furnished and semi-furnished properties one of the biggest questions is what do you leave in the unit. Many times the decision depends on how expensive it is to move a particular item. This is especially true when you are renting out a home or condo that you were unable to sell.

For example, it may cost more to move the 15-year-old non-energy efficient side-by-side refrigerator/freezer than it would to replace the item outright. If you are moving out of this place to another home you may also want to furnish the new place with new appliances.

Another issue may be items that are long past their useful lives or are broken. That overstuffed recliner that has seen ten years of stains and rugged use may not make a prospective tenant want to rent from you. That dishwasher that only works occasionally will cause endless complaints from your tenant and will ruin the relationship between you and the tenant. You want your rental to look appealing, to have everything in working order, and to be move-in clean.

Nothing of any sentimental value should be left in the rental. This is not the place for grandma's antique rocker, dad's homemade bar, or a china cabinet full of dishes. No matter how kind or nice the tenants are, they do not want to be custodians for your museum.

THE PROPERTY ITSELF

Once you have decided what you are leaving in the rental, it is time to clean.

Entire Rental Area

Repair cracks or blemishes in the wall with paint, wallpaper, or tile. Clean all glass. Wipe down walls with cleaning solution. Clean curtains and rugs. Wipe out the insides of drawers, cabinets, and closets. A good product to use is a spray pine cleaner that will leave a clean scent.

Bathrooms

Toss out all old toiletry containers. Scrub the toilet, tub, and sink. Use tile cleaning products on the tile and lime cleaning products on faucets and places with rust or lime stains. Check caulking around tub/shower, sink, and toilet. If it is loose or broken get an inexpensive tube of caulk and repair it. Leave at least one full roll of toilet paper, even if the unit is rented unfurnished.

Kitchen

Clean the top of the stove and the oven. Clean inside the dishwasher and refrigerator with products made for the appliance. Wipe down tops of cabinets. If countertops require a special cleaner, be sure to leave a container of that cleaner with the tenants. Leave at least one full roll of paper towels, even if the unit is rented unfurnished.

Renting Out Your Vacation Home

If you have a vacation home, be it a cabin or sleek condo in a vacation area, you may want to consider renting it out as a way to make some money. This chapter discusses renting out vacation homes, problems you may have along the way, how you should prepare your property, and what to do to make your rental wow the competition.

ASSOCIATIONS

How Associations Can Impact Your Rental

If your vacation property is a condo, in a multi-unit building, in a gated area, or in any way governed by an association, make sure that you are legally able to rent out your property. (This check is in addition to checking the city, county, and state laws that rentals must follow.) Any governing body, including a condo association, community association, co-op association, or resort association can prevent you from renting out your property and/or charge you fees for doing so.

It is not unusual in a resort or vacation area for the association/resort owner to require that all rentals be handled through the association/ resort office. This is done so that one irresponsible tenant or inattentive landlord does not negatively impact the rest of the units. It may also give the association a piece of the lucrative rental market.

For the owners of the units, this arrangement can provide a built-in property manager.

Make sure that you look at any association agreement that you signed when you purchased the property. That agreement may have a clause that escalates your association fees or requires an additional fee if anyone other than the owner uses the property.

How Associations Can Help Your Rental

Sometimes an association or resort office can be very useful when you decide to rent out your vacation property. Your association may be able to act as the property manger for your vacation property. The association may offer services such as tenant screening, preparing the property, property repair, maid service, or rent collection. Yes, you will probably pay a fee for those services, but it will probably be less than having to arrange all these services with other businesses. In addition, if your vacation rental is in another state the association's services will save you time and the expense of transportation to your rental to take care of these tasks.

If your property is not part of an association, you may want to look for someone to act as an on-site property manager or at least to handle emergency calls from the tenant when something breaks on the property. Some real estate firms in resort areas offer services as property managers. These services may even include marketing your property to prospective renters.

Each individual landlord must decide how much he or she wants to be involved with the vacation rental. A lot depends on how far away that rental is from his or her home. If it is a fishing cabin that is a three-hour drive away, the landlord may decide to handle everything. The same may not be true for an elegant vacation condo in an expensive resort town that requires a two-hour flight.

When looking for assistance/property management for your vacation property look first to any association or group that the property is part of. Second, look to professionals in the area such as real estate firms. Finally, look to individuals that can be hired to perform certain tasks.

COMMON PROBLEMS IN VACATION RENTALS

If you are not lucky enough to have built-in property managers for your vacation rental you will need to follow the procedures listed earlier in this book, especially the part about screening tenants. Sometimes the owners of vacation homes can be a bit lax about tenant screening. Tenants who cause problems in your vacation home can cost you at the time the damage is done, and, worse, if you rent to several tenants over a season, one bad tenant can cause a loss of income for the entire season. Because a vacation home is usually fully furnished it is very important that you collect a sufficient amount of deposit money up front to pay for broken or stolen furnishings.

Another major issue you will need to think about is insurance. You should contact your property insurance agent if you are planning to rent out your vacation property. There may be additional riders that need to be put on your current policy to protect the property from tenant disasters. Your property insurance agent may be able to give you pointers on how to prepare your property with an eye toward safety and property protection.

Furnishing a Vacation Rental

Vacation rentals are usually totally furnished. This includes kitchen utensils, bed linens, and necessities such as toilet paper.

The very first issue should be safety. Even if your local laws do not require it, your vacation rental should have a smoke detector and carbon monoxide detector on every level, a kitchen fire extinguisher, and a fire extinguisher in any outside cooking area. Make a laminated sheet with directions for turning off the main water and main gas connection, for dealing with electrical failures (fuses or breakers), and that lists important phone numbers (police, fire, electric company, gas company, how to reach you).

If tile or countertops require special cleaning materials be sure to provide them. If the septic system needs a certain type of toilet paper make sure there is a sufficient quantity of that type in the rental.

As for decorating, go for casual, easy to keep clean, non-staining items that are comfortable. If you are renting out a vacation home or condo, do not over-decorate or decorate with pricey antiques that may grow legs and walk away. Vacation tenants consider a good bed with several good bed pillows and blankets to be necessities. Other must-haves are a good coffee maker, a toaster, an alarm clock, and plenty of towels. As a common courtesy make sure that the rental has plenty of paper towels, toilet paper, extra light bulbs, and an area phone book. Many vacation rental landlords also leave flyers for local restaurants, directions to local attractions, and information on the surrounding area.

Because this is a vacation rental you can get by with classy indoor/outdoor furniture, which is less expensive to replace than indoor-only furniture. We are not talking about aluminum tube folding chairs with the web strips, though. Look at faux-wicker furniture that comes with removable cushions for the couch, chairs, and ottomans. For dining, look at glass and metal tables (with or without a hole for an umbrella) and matching chairs. The best part of selecting indoor/outdoor furniture is if your tenants drag the couch outside, the rain and sun will not hurt it.

The Competition

We all have seen ads on TV for elegant time-shares and beautiful apartments in fantastic resort areas. If you are renting out a vacation home, that is your competition. Even if your vacation rental is nowhere near that fantastic resort area, prospective tenants see these ads on TV and expect all vacation rentals to look the same.

With the abundance of vacation rentals, you may find yourself catering to renters who are a bit spoiled. It is not unusual for rentals in high-end resort towns to include plasma TVs, wireless Internet hook up, expensive bathrobes, and other expensive amenities. Look at what other rentals in your area are offering. You can find them in local newspapers or on the websites that list vacation rentals. Your rental may have other attributes that make it unnecessary to include the high-end goodies. Many vacationers are more interested in a relaxing place away from the city that has quiet and privacy, than in fancy bathrobes.

Property Insurance

This chapter covers the dry and sometimes mundane subject of property insurance for rental property. This is another of the very important issues that must be individually tailored to meet the needs of the landlord and the individual property. Your best advisor about how much and what type of coverage your property will need is the insurance provider that you already have your homeowners insurance with.

RULES OF PROTECTING YOUR RENTAL PROPERTY

- Do not leave anything in the rental unit that you will be unable to replace. Take out the artwork and mom's dishes.

- Pre-screen tenants. Rent to those who have a history of being good tenants.

- Require a damage deposit to cover damage to the property and items stolen.

✪   Do an inventory of everything left in the property and take pictures of the condition of the property. Have the tenant sign off on both, acknowledging that the property was in this condition when it was rented.

✪   Finally, have sufficient property insurance to take care of major damages and disasters.

TURNING YOUR HOMEOWNERS INSURANCE INTO INSURANCE FOR YOUR RENTAL PROPERTY

Having sufficient property insurance on a rental property is not merely a luxury, it is a must. Property insurance protects your investment. This is one item that you must not neglect.

Obtaining a sufficient amount of property insurance is one place where you will need the expertise of another professional—your insurance agent or broker. Your insurance agent or broker is trained to understand the very complex subject of insurance policies and how they apply to actual structures. Use your insurance professional to help you pick out the appropriate coverage for your rental.

If you are renting out a property that has not previously been used as a rental, contact your current homeowners insurance agent or broker. Let the agent know that you are now planning to use the property as a rental. Many of the larger insurance companies have materials to assist property owners in determining how much insurance to purchase and advising what can be done to the property to keep it safe.

Landlords should make sure the insurance coverage protects the value of the property. As property values increase so should the amount of insurance coverage. The best type of policy is one that includes coverage for physical injuries, libel, slander, discrimination, wrongful evictions, and invasion of privacy suffered by tenants and guests, along with coverage for the perils of storm damage, water, fire, wind, lightning, and arson. Encourage your tenants to carry renters insurance. The renters policy should cover not only the tenant's property but damage and injuries caused by the tenant or the tenant's guests to other tenants, their guests, other rental units, and the property itself.

The purchase of insurance on property is not a matter of finding the cheapest policy. A landlord should look at the services that the insurance company will provide, the responsiveness of this company in paying claims, the expertise that the agent/broker has in dealing with rental property, and the willingness to work with the landlord to protect the insured property. If the insurance agent/broker is not willing to take the time to answer questions from the landlord or assist the landlord in determining how much insurance to purchase, the landlord should find another insurance agent/broker.

Many times the best price for insurance coverage on rental property can be obtained through the insurance company that also insures your car, your home, and your business. Insurance companies will usually give a good deal to property owners who insure multiple items with the same company.

TENANT INSURANCE

We discuss insurance taken out by the tenant, or what is commonly called renters insurance, in several places in this book. Renters insurance is a policy that will protect the tenant when the tenant has damages to his or her property. Nowadays tenants come armed with expensive computers and all variety of extremely expensive electronics. Should there be a stray lightning bolt or some other electrical surge, that tenant can lose all that expensive equipment in a blink of an eye. Many renters insurance policies will protect that equipment. These policies can also protect the tenant if his or her property is damaged by fire, wind, or an incident caused by another tenant. Renters insurance may also protect the tenant if his or her actions cause damage to the landlord's property or another tenant's property.

For example, if a tenant in a multi-unit building starts a fire in the kitchen of his unit and the fire expands upward, destroying all the property of the upstairs tenants and causing water damage to the property of the downstairs tenants, the landlord's insurance covers the structural repairs on the building, but, unless the landlord's insurance has additional riders to the policy, the tenants are responsible for their own losses of personal property. The upstairs and downstairs tenants may have a cause of action to sue the tenant that started the fire. However, that tenant has lost everything also so he or she probably will not be able to get anything. It is for this type of situation that renters insurance will be an asset. Depending on the policy and the facts in the case, the renter's insurance may be able to reimburse other tenants and possibly the landlord should it be determined that the fire was deliberately started.

When you arrange your property insurance, ask your insurance agent/ broker about the availability of renters insurance. Your insurance professional will be able to explain how your tenants will benefit from this type of policy. Your insurance professional may also be able to provide you with brochures or other information to pass on to your tenants, along with an approximation of the cost of such a policy. This can be one more service that you provide to your tenants.

Putting Your Property on the Market

Marketing is the bane of all business owners. How much do you spend on advertising? Where do you advertise? To whom do you appeal? Let's face it, where you advertise will determine the type of tenant that you will get. This is the one area where a landlord can be discriminating without being illegally discriminatory.

ADVERTISING DECISIONS

Marketing or advertising your product is a series of decisions that will present your property to the right people. In determining details that will be presented in your advertising, begin with the following:

- ✪ What type of rental do I want? Rent to own? Annual rental? Month-to-month?

- ✪ What stays with the property? Fully furnished? Semi-furnished? Unfurnished?

- ✪ What type of rental property do I have? One unit/condo? Full house?

✪ What are the assets of this property? Spa bathroom? Washer and dryer in the unit? Common area with pool? Single family home? Has commercial property attached? Includes boat launch?

✪ What are the assets of the area? Close to downtown transportation? Walking distance to university, hospital, parks, senior center, town, high school, grade school, shopping? Quiet neighborhood? Access to public transportation?

Where to Advertise/ Market

Another big decision is where you want to advertise your property. This can have a great effect on who will respond to your ad. For example, if you are renting out a vacation home/condo you will want to appeal to a different group of tenants than if you have a rental property that is close to a university. Here are some ideas on places to market your rental:

For all rentals:

✪ Place an ad in the local paper.

✪ Where local businesses allow, put an ad in their lobbies.

✪ Place an ad in flyers that concentrate on rentals.

✪ Put an ad in reputable Internet forums.

✪ Some real estate agencies will list your rental for a modest fee.

In addition, for vacation rentals:

✪ Place an ad in a vacation newsletter.

✪ If your vacation area has its own website, advertising brochures, or publicity, advertise in these.

✪ List your rental with travel agents.

✪ Create your own website with an online tour of the property.

In addition, for rentals near universities:

- Place an ad in the college newspaper.

- Offer short-term rentals (for the semester).

- List your rental with the university.

Of course, if you have a property manager, he or she may handle the market of your rental property without you lifting a finger.

Free Marketing   Yes, there are such things as free or at least low-cost marketing. You may be able to put a free ad in bulletins from your church, your civic groups, your local club, or your employer. If you are Internet proficient, create a blog, or build a website where you can post your information. Some grocery stores let their customers put up small ads in the exit area of the store. There are also charities that will allow an ad to be purchased in their newsletter. Your town may also have a newsletter or local information directory that will offer low-cost ads.

WRITING ADS

How do you word the advertisement? Each region of the county has its own colloquial terms for describing property. You can learn how to set up an advertisement by reading the current rental ads for your area. Also, the media that you use to advertise in may have their own formats of what should be listed in an ad.

At a minimum, you want to include information that answers the most common questions of prospective tenants and provide a phone number for interested parties to call. Providing important information such as number of bedrooms, rental cost, and area of the city eliminates phone calls from people who just want more information.

You also want to provide some comment that will generate interest in your property. Tell prospective tenants why they should rent your property. Let them know what special features or assets make your rental better than the next. For example:

- close to the University of _____;

- within walking distance to downtown;

- has a security entrance system;

- has twenty-four-hour doorman;

- underground parking included;

- health club on premises;

- in the heart of the financial district;

- extra storage space provided;

- granite countertops in kitchen and bath; and

- gourmet kitchen.

WHO DO YOU WANT TO ATTRACT?

A major part of marketing is determining who you want to appeal to. This is especially important when you are looking for tenants.

Let's be honest, we all have a prejudices. For most landlords this does not have anything to do with racism or hatred of a certain religion, it is an issue of protecting your property and your other tenants. However, there are laws in effect that strictly limit what you can say in a marketing ad for tenants—no matter how good your intentions are.

Using Euphemisms to Attract the Right Tenants

A euphemism is a word or phrase that means something other than its literal definition. For example, we used to call the men who picked up our trash garbage men, but they are now referred to as sanitation engineers. The best industry for not only making up euphemisms but for using them in marketing is the real estate industry. Just look at the ads for home sales. Where else but the real estate industry can a phrase such as "cute dollhouse" mean too much clutter in a small area, or a phrase such as "handyman's delight" mean a structure that may fall down any second.

Using Terms That Do Not Discriminate

Some people use euphemisms and slang expressions in a manner that is illegal discrimination. There have been many instances where a particular euphemism was put in an ad for housing to direct a certain race or ethnicity away from that area. That is illegal. Tenants nowadays are smart in the ways of discrimination, and if the landlord markets in a discriminatory manner it will be uncovered. Discrimination is illegal and expensive to litigate, so please keep that in mind when phrasing your ads.

The vast majority of landlords do not want to discriminate, but they do want a tenant who will respect the property and hopefully fit in with the other tenants. So the landlord needs to fully describe the property in terms that take full advantage of the multiple meaning words.

What Does Family Mean?

A big example of how the media uses euphemisms in ads is the word *family*. A place to bring your family, family friendly atmosphere, family oriented town, a movie for the family. Family has come to mean that children are welcomed, children will not be exposed to adult words, we like children.

However, the word family is a prime example of how euphemisms can have different meanings to different types of people. Take the restaurant that advertises, "Great place for families." The restaurant wants to express to customers that they welcome the customers' children, and they may have smaller child portions and ample booster-chairs. The restaurant wants to convey the feeling of a family meal in a not-so-fussy atmosphere where everyone is welcome.

A person with children who reads that ad may pick up on the restaurant's intent and consider that restaurant as a place where he or she can bring his or her children for a good meal. However, for people who no longer have young children, who are childfree, or who are looking for a quiet place to have a meal with a special someone, this same ad may scream "Stay Away/A Place Where Screaming Kids Are Welcome/ You Will Feel Out of Place Here."

When writing an ad the landlord must keep in mind that even the most neutral term implies things to people. Each word in an ad must be carefully selected.

Appealing to the Tenants You Want

For a rental property where the landlord specifically wants to welcome a family with children, the landlord could advertise it as being close to a specific grade school, on the route of a bus service to a particular high school, or close to several day care centers. For a multi-unit building, the landlord may say that there is a playground on the premises, or plenty of room for a family to play.

But what happens if the property that the landlord is renting out is not so family friendly. Maybe all of the other tenants are senior citizens, or the property would not be a good fit for younger children because of its proximity to a railroad or other hazard. Then the ad could say the property is close to a local senior center, that there is free bus service to a particular medical center, or that it is within walking distance to a medical center.

More examples:

Ad states "This property is close to..."	Landlord is looking for:
the senior center	senior citizens
local grade school	family with young children
local high school	family with older children
top-notch day care facility	single parents who work
medical facilities/hospital	senior citizens, hospital workers
university	students, young adults
public transportation	those who are at work all day
bars, nightlife, theatre	young adults
airport	airline workers, travelers

In summary, a landlord needs to determine what type of tenants he or she is looking for. Then the landlord should advertise to that group by crafting an ad that plays up the positives of the property and the neighborhood in terms your target group of tenants will find enticing.

SECTION 7

TENANTS—PART 1 THE GOOD

In this section we look at the person who will rent your property, the tenant. The vast majority of tenants are good people who need a roof over their heads and are willing to pay a fair rent amount. The worst thing that can be said about these people is that they sometimes may need a bit of education and guidance from a fair and just landlord.

We begin by helping the landlord screen tenants. While the screening process may look cumbersome, it is meant to protect the landlord from potential housing discrimination claims and to assist the landlord in finding the right tenant.

Next we cover a very important issue in today's economy, tenants with companion animals. It is no longer standard for landlords to prevent companion animals. Landlords have found that tenants who care for pets are also the type of people that care for property. Furthermore, landlords are finding that allowing pets gives them a larger pool of tenants to choose from and puts their property ahead of many other rentals on the market.

Finally we look at moving in the selected tenant—last minute preparation of the property, and what a landlord can do to begin a harmonious relationship with the tenant.

Screening Tenants

This chapter discusses the most important duty of a landlord, picking the right tenant. Your tenant has the power to make being a landlord a wonderful or a hellish experience. Tenants can cause damages to property that costs thousands of dollars to repair or they can leave the property in better shape than it was when they moved in. Tenants can also cost the landlord thousands of dollars in legal fees and litigation expenses.

This chapter is about the methods and tools used to find the right tenant for your rental property. Unfortunately, bad tenants do not wear signs or have a certain look about them; anyone can be a bad tenant. It is up to the landlord to use available tools to determine if a person is likely to be a good tenant. No set of tools is foolproof, but here we present what is currently available for the landlord to utilize in making a decision.

In addition, in this chapter we are introducing a system for handling prospective tenants. This is a paper system that will provide the landlord with the appropriate records and procedures to combat any claims of discrimination in renting.

MEETING WITH PROSPECTIVE TENANTS

If you have done the proper marketing of your rental property you should soon be receiving calls from people who want to look at the property and possibly rent it. Because the potential for discrimination begins when the prospective tenant makes the first contact, the landlord and his or her staff need to be careful when dealing with prospective tenants on the phone. Information such as number of rooms, location of unit, monthly rent, and the physical attributes of the rental should be provided to anyone who calls. However, never answer the question "Will you rent this place to me?" with a yes or no. Ask all prospective tenants to fill out a rental application. Tell the prospective tenant that once the application is made and credit checks and employment checks are made, you can then answer that question.

If you are renting out a vacation home, both the prospective tenant and the landlord may live far away from the rental property and each other. In that case the landlord must rely on phone calls and faxed and mailed forms filled out by the prospective tenant to determine if the person will make a good tenant.

NOTE: *If you have hired a property manager, he or she probably will handle the tenant screening and you may never speak with a prospective tenant. However, a landlord should be aware of what goes on in tenant screenings in order to make sure that there is no illegal discrimination.*

Discrimination   In addition to finding a suitable tenant, the landlord must be wary about the issue of housing discrimination. This concern begins when the prospective tenant contacts the landlord, the property manager, or the landlord's staff. Obvious acts that discourage a prospective tenant from renting a property due to the tenant's race, religion, nationality, sex, age, or any other basis of discrimination that is set out by the federal law or your state's laws can cause the prospective tenant to file a complaint against the landlord—even if the tenant never actually rents from this landlord. Common things that courts consider as evidence of discrimination against a prospective tenant include:

✪   The landlord refuses to show a prospective tenant the rental (tenant alleges that it is because of his or her race, and the landlord must prove that he or she has shown the rental to members of that race).

✪ The landlord tells a prospective tenant that he or she will not feel right in this rental because it is "not for your kind of people," or because the tenant would be "the only one of his or her kind in the building," or because "it would upset my other tenants if I rent to you."

✪ The landlord treats a prospective tenant in any manner that is different than the treatment of other prospective tenants. (For example, the landlord gives only prospective tenants of a certain race or nationality flyers on the landlord's anti-gang policy, the landlord restricts certain minorities in the number of people that can live in a unit, or the landlord does a credit check on only certain minorities.) All rules must be equally applied to every prospective tenant, and the landlord must be able to prove that this is the procedure used.

You should review specific laws against discrimination, especially the local fair housing law in your particular city. In general, all fair housing laws say it is illegal to refuse to rent to someone because of that person's race, religion, ethnic origin, sex, age, because of children (except in senior housing), or due to a disability. Some states and cities also preclude discrimination based on a prospective tenant's marital status, sexual orientation, or other issues.

A landlord can legally select tenants based on sound business reasons such as insufficient income, poor credit history, and past behavior in rental property (such as damaging rental units, evictions, complaints). A landlord can also create a valid rule as to the number of people living in a single unit as long as that rule can be clearly justified on the basis of health and safety.

THE PROSPECTIVE TENANT SYSTEM

As a landlord you or your property manager cannot, by law, discriminate when renting property. (See Section 3 for more on Housing Discrimination laws.) As stated above, charges of discrimination commonly stem from prospective tenants who file a complaint with the proper authorities alleging that they were discriminated against and were unable to rent a property because of illegal discrimination.

These types of charges are both costly and time-consuming to defend against. In most cases the landlord is required to produce past records of how prospective tenants were treated, what prospective tenants were told, and the reasons that some prospective tenants were rejected. Landlords who do not keep proper records or who have not written down the criteria that they judge all prospective tenants on can get caught up in a he said/she said allegation that ends up causing needless and expensive litigation.

We are introducing the following system to help the landlord by making the paperwork provided to all prospective tenants the same and by setting up procedures for handling all prospective tenants, creating a paper trail that the landlord can turn over to a court if necessary.

Prospective Tenant Master List (form 03 001)

This is a list of every prospective tenant who has contacted the landlord regarding renting the landlord's property, along with the following information:

- ✪ first date the prospective tenant contacted you;

- ✪ the prospective tenant's name;

- ✪ the prospective tenant's contact info, including a phone number where the person can be reached;

- ✪ the date the prospective tenant filled out and returned an application;

- ✪ whether the prospective tenant's application was accepted or rejected; and

- ✪ the date the acceptance or rejection was communicated to the prospective tenant.

The Prospective Tenant Master List should be kept in a binder, separate from other prospective tenant materials. If the landlord has a staff, the staff should be instructed to record the date, the name, and contact info of anyone who is interested in renting from this landlord. All prospective tenants should be given an envelope containing information on the rental, a rental application, and any other forms the landlord requires. The prospective tenant must fill out and return the application and forms so that the landlord can determine if this person meets the guidelines for tenants.

Prospective Tenant Kit

Use a large envelope to hold the materials that will be given to all prospective tenants. For efficiency, make up several of these envelopes so that you can quickly provide the same information to each prospective tenant. Instruct your staff to hand each prospective tenant one of these packets after they have shown the prospective tenant the rental unit and the prospective tenant indicates that he or she is interested in renting.

This envelope should include:

- a form letter to the prospective tenant asking the prospective tenant to fill out rental application and permission forms, and lets the prospective tenant know that all tenants go through this process (form 03 002, p.267);

- a rental application (form 03 003, p.268);

- a statement regarding non-discrimination (form 03 004, p.269);

- permission forms for a credit check and an employment check (form 03 005, p.270); and

- a summary of important rules for tenants or a copy of all the rules for this rental property (form 03 006, p.271).

Samples of each of these materials are in the Forms section of this book. You may want to make certain adjustments on these forms to match the laws within your state.

NOTE: *If you are renting out your home because you were not able to sell it, the above seems like a lot of busywork. You still need to do it. As a landlord of even one property you are subject to the same discrimination laws as landlords with multiple properties. If tossed into a discrimination complaint you will need to prove the same things as landlords of multi-unit structures. Even when you rent out one home you will still need to have the prospective tenant fill out an application and you will want to provide the tenant with rules. The beauty of this system is that it does not necessarily require a computer, although it could be easily adapted in any word processing software. You can copy the Master List form in the back of this book, and you can use inexpensive envelopes from the Dollar Store. While it may seem cumbersome, if you are caught up in a discrimination complaint you will be grateful that you have all the information in one spot.*

WHAT HAPPENS AFTER THE PROSPECTIVE TENANT RETURNS THE APPLICATIONS AND FORMS?

The prospective tenant must return a rental application that is fully filled out, and signed permission forms for credit checks, employment checks, and reference checks. Those who refuse to provide the information required or to sign any of the permission forms should be rejected.

Courts have also determined that it is not illegal for the landlord to ask prospective tenants for the following:

✪ social security number;

✪ bank account information;

✪ driver's license number;

✪ release to do a credit check;

✪ release to do an employment check;

✪   criminal history;

✪   character references; and

✪   number of anticipated visitors.

Of course, your state may have prohibitions on what a landlord can ask the prospective tenant, which is why you need to locate and understand your local laws on landlord/tenant relationships.

Prospective tenants can refuse to answer questions on the rental application. However, the landlord is under no legal obligation to rent to prospective tenants who refuse to answer any questions as long as these questions are part of the screening process that all prospective tenants must go through.

EVALUATING THE RENTAL APPLICATION

Each landlord must set up his or her own criteria for evaluating prospective tenants. It is a good idea to write the criteria down so that you and your staff can reference it and use it for potential court fights.

The criteria must be in accord with federal, state, and local laws. It should not contain any discriminatory terms or methods for discrimination against a prospective tenant. The criteria should be focused on what is considered a true business need—can this person pay the rent, will this person take care of the property, will this person follow the rental rules, will this person be an annoyance to other tenants, is this person truthful in his or her application, will this person follow the local laws and the rules of the property.

The financial questions surrounding a prospective tenant are usually answered by three methods: 1) running a credit check on the prospective tenant; 2) contacting the tenant's current employer regarding salary; and 3) checking with the tenant's former landlord and references.

There is nothing in federal law that prohibits the landlord from charging for obtaining credit reports on prospective tenants as long as credit reports are required for all prospective tenants and the same amount is charged to each prospective tenant. Landlords should check for any local laws that address this issue.

THE DECISION

Once the landlord has evaluated the rental application and the other material regarding the prospective tenant, a decision needs to be made. Some landlords stall at this point, not wanting to give bad news. However, it is important that the landlord handle this promptly and professionally. It may be preferable that the landlord send a neutral form letter to the rejected tenant informing the person of the decision. See form 03 007, p.272.

The landlord should note on the rental application the decision and the reasons. For those prospective tenants who are not selected, this rental application should be kept as a record should the landlord need to provide evidence on tenant evaluations.

For tenants who pass the application process, the landlord needs to contact them and provide an acceptance conditioned on the tenant providing the appropriate amount of money up front and signing the lease. See form 03 008, p.273.

chapter 23

Tenants with Companion Animals

The issue of pets in rentals is important to both the landlord and the tenant. For many tenants, a pet or companion animal can be a friend, or even a part of the family. As our society continues on its separation trend where family members rarely live in the same state and friends are on a computer screen, perhaps thousands of miles away, our companion animals become our anchors.

On the downside, from a landlord's point of view, a pet can damage the property, can annoy other tenants, and, at worst, can cause a lawsuit that involves the landlord. However, landlords should not automatically bar all pets; there are ways to satisfy the needs of both landlord and tenants on the issue of companion animals.

LAWS ABOUT COMPANION ANIMALS

Federal law makes it a civil rights violation to refuse to rent to a person because that person has a guide, hearing, or support dog. This is considered discrimination and a landlord who refuses to rent to a tenant with a service dog is subject to a discrimination complaint. The majority of state laws also require landlords to allow service dogs. These laws are usually under the Americans with Disabilities Act (ADA).

In some states, if a person can prove a special need for a companion animal, the "No Pets" clause in a lease can successfully be challenged in court. This type of case very often involves an autistic child who benefits from the presence of the animal. Tenants who have won these types of court cases have been able to prove that the companion animal is necessary because of a physical or an emotional condition, that the animal is required for health and well-being, and that they would suffer if they were forced to give up their animals. This testimony is usually backed up by testimony from the tenant's doctors and experts in the field of companion animals who cite studies that show companion animals will lower blood pressure, improve self-esteem, and in general improve a tenant's overall health.

There are some civil cases, which have yet to enter the appeal stage, of other groups of tenants who are fighting to be able to have companion animals in a rental. These new groups include both children and adults who have been medically diagnosed with depression and the elderly. For tenants with depression, the argument is that there is a medical necessity for the companion animal. While this is the same argument that is advanced for the elderly, in the case of the elderly the diagnosis is not limited to depression but includes an overall quality of life. These cases are being brought under the Americans with Disabilities Act, which our government has recently expanded. There are many supporters of allowing companion animals, and even the National Institutes of Health, a prestigious scientific agency, has found evidence to support the finding that pets are medically beneficial to some people's health.

A few states have allowed a companion animal in rentals with "No Pets" rules due to security issues. The tenant asserts that the animal is needed as security in a rental property where there is a history of break-ins. These types of cases are rare and are not handled the same in every state. However, all states are lending a sympathetic ear to tenants with companion animals who have been forced out of their homes by disasters such as Katrina, flooding in the Midwest, or earthquakes, or those forced out of their homes by foreclosure.

There are, of course, laws against animal abuse and procedures about liability when there is a dog bite. Municipalities may have local ordinances that restrict the number of animals in a rental property, that allow a tenant to keep an animal that has been with the tenant for a period of time, or that prohibit a landlord from changing a lease to "No Pets" without a specified notice. Continuous, loud dog barking my also violate a local noise ordinance.

PET OWNERS AS TENANTS

In a survey done by the San Francisco SPCA, it was found that pet owners were more stable tenants. Landlords who permit pets see their vacancy rates drop, there is a larger pool of prospective tenants, and tenants are more happy and satisfied. Furthermore, tenants who take the responsibility to care for pets properly are often more responsible in taking care of the rental property. Responsible pet owners do clean up after their animals and repair damages that their animals cause. The question for landlords is, "How do you find pet owners who are responsible?"

FINDING RESPONSIBLE PET OWNERS

Just like finding responsible tenants, finding responsible pet owners means a little more work for the landlord. But with a weakened economy and an abundance of rental housing on the market, a landlord will be required to do a bit of extra work in order to expand the pool of potential tenants anyway. Directing that extra work at a group of tenants who are known for responsibility is just good business.

The landlord may want to get assistance from the many organizations that are devoted to animals. In many cities the local shelters, anti-cruelty offices, and/or humane treatment of animals offices are actively helping match landlords who will rent to those with companion animals with tenants. Some of these premier organizations will provide the landlord with free advertising on the organization's website, will screen the prospective tenant, and will provide guaranteed assistance to the tenant or a variety of other services that keep companion animals with responsible tenants and off the streets. This is a very good deal for the landlord, who can actually save money by using these services. Many of these organizations will also work with tenants to teach them to become responsible pet owners not just before the rental but as an ongoing resource to the landlords.

Local pet stores may also be able to assist the landlord by providing another place to put up free ads for tenants. Many of these pet stores will be thrilled to get a relationship with a landlord who rents to those with companion animals. This store can advise the landlord on the right type of cleaning products for the property before and after the tenant with companion animal rents. Pet stores and pet supercenters are also a wealth of information on pet behavioral problems and places that provide obedience training for dogs. In addition to food, many of these stores stock the tools needed to pick up after an animal. In addition, once the landlord builds a relationship with such a store the tenants may be eligible for discounts—another plus for your property.

The best way to find responsible pet owners as tenants is:

- ✪ Set up an additional procedure for screening tenants who want to bring their companion animals into the rental property. This procedure should include interviewing the prospective tenant regarding the pet, verifying that the pet is up to date on all required vaccinations, contacting any former landlords who dealt with this pet, and possibly contacting the veterinarian who sees the pet regarding aggression or other negative traits (form 09 001, p.285).

- ✪ Set up rules for tenants with pets. These rules can be very detailed and must be enforced equally for all tenants (form 09 002, p.286).

- ✪ Require that tenants register each pet. This registration includes contact information for the veterinarian that has cares for this pet. Along with the current veterinarian, the tenant must prove that this animal is up to date on all required vaccinations.

- ✪ Require that tenants pay an additional security deposit for each pet. This deposit goes directly to removal of animal smells and damage done by the animal.

INTERVIEWING PROSPECTIVE TENANTS WITH COMPANION ANIMALS

The first step comes in the interview of the potential tenant. Once a property is listed as "Pets OK" there should be no shortage of prospective tenants. In the interview the landlord should ask the following:

✪ How long have you had the pet?

✪ Have there been any complaints about your pets at your current address? If so, how did you resolve those complaints?

✪ Did your pet cause any damage at your current address? If so, did you pay for the damage?

✪ May we contact your current landlord to discuss your pet further?

✪ Who will care for your pet when you are away on vacation or business?

✪ Would you object to my periodically checking on your pet to note any damage and to see how the pet is adjusting?

✪ Has your pet been spayed or neutered?

✪ Does your cat use a litter box?

✪ Do you have a regular veterinarian?

✪ Is your pet up to date on his or her shots? License?

✪ Does your animal have any medical or behavior problems? If so, what treatment/training is it receiving?

✪ How does your pet get along with other animals and people?

✪ How much time will your animal spend alone each day?

WHY HAVE RULES FOR TENANTS WITH PETS?

The purpose of having rules for pet owners is to keep property damage to a minimum and allow all tenants the quiet enjoyment of the property as required by law. Be realistic in rules. Both dogs and cats can cause damage; pet owners should be on notice that any damage done by their pets will be charged to them.

Dogs   Dog owners must clean up after their dogs as soon as the dog defecates. Most local laws require that all dog walkers carry and use a pooper-scooper or other method of removing the dog's solid waste. Building owners may wish to designate a portion of their property for dog walking or as a dog run. Dogs should be spayed or neutered. Female dogs in heat can attack other animals, be noisy, and attract persistent suitors.

Determine how big a dog to allow in a rental unit. Many giant dogs such as Great Danes and mastiffs are laid-back, easygoing types that can live quite happily in an apartment as long as they are given daily exercise, while more active breeds such as border collies and some spaniels may require more exercise than can be given in one or two daily walks. It depends on the dog, which is one reason for the landlord needs to ask questions about the dog and perhaps even meet with the dog and owner prior to renting.

A note here about the elderly dog: because many people are losing their homes due to foreclosure it is not unusual for the landlord to have a potential tenant with an elderly or sick dog that would normally not qualify under the weight/height/breed rules. Please have a heart in this situation. That poor animal probably will not last very long. To force a person to decide between his or her elderly, sick dog and a place to live is horribly unfair. For many of us, the illness and death of our beloved companion animal is as painful as the loss of a child. Let compassion, not rules, guide you.

Cats   For cats, tenants must provide a sufficient number of litter boxes. Usually each cat must have its own box. Cats that are spayed and neutered usually do not spray urine, and cats kept indoors do not have the opportunity to leave urine marks on lawns. Therefore, a landlord may want to require that all cats be spayed or neutered.

It is a myth that cats must be free to roam. In our cities this ignorant myth has cost the lives of millions of beautiful, loving domesticated cats that were someone's sweet companion. Most cats, once spayed or neutered, no longer have the need to go out and hunt. Domestic cats adapt very well to being kept indoors, and will live longer and healthier lives as a result.

There is nothing more heartbreaking than seeing a cat that has been hit by a car. Tenants with cats should be required to keep the cat in the rental unit at all times, a rule that includes not being allowed on balconies without a leash. Cats allowed on balconies or outside can easily adapt to walking on a leash or harness or riding in the latest product for pets, the pet stroller. The landlord should make sure that there are secure screens in all windows for the safety of cats, not to mention children and adults.

Common Pet Issues   The age of the pet can be a factor in deciding whether to rent to a prospective tenant with a pet. A young puppy is an unknown quantity, it may be crying during the night for feedings, just like a human baby does. Older dogs and older cats tend to be less active, but they also can be crabby and set in their ways. Older animals can be a problem if the landlord decides to set up a no-pets rule in a building where pets were previously permitted. Older animals have almost no chance to be adopted from humane shelters where the tenants surrender their animal. Also, the media and animal activists will pounce on a story of a 90-year-old widow forced to give up her 20-year-old cat, and the publicity will not be good for the landlord.

Some pets can suffer from separation anxiety or become bored and destructive when left alone for periods of time, like the typical ten hours a day when their owner goes to work. Cats typically sleep sixteen hours a day or more, but some dogs may bark, chew, whine, or indulge in destructive behavior. For a prospective tenant who has had the animal for a period of time, this separation anxiety should be known and he or she should have some solutions for this problem. Sometimes such an animal needs additional exercise, professional training, or the addition of another animal for company.

As for repairing animal damage, it would be best if any damage can be spotted before it becomes extensive. This may mean periodic inspections of a rental unit, enforcing a rule on litter boxes, even making materials for cleaning up pet messes available to pet owners. There are many chain pet stores that stock professional animal odor neutralizers, pooper-scoopers, and other items to clean up after an animal. A landlord may be able to work a deal with the local pet store to provide both education and products to the tenants.

EXAMPLES OF RULES FOR TENANT PET OWNERS

The landlord should set up rules specifically for pet owners. These should be shown to the prospective tenant during the interview so that if there is any problem abiding by these rules the landlord can know up front. These rules should then be incorporated into the lease by a clause incorporating the document, "Rules for Tenant Pet Owners," into the lease. Using an incorporation clause allows the landlord to change the rules without changing the lease.

The following are common rules for tenant pet owners:

Specifically for Those with Dogs

- ✪ Limit the number of dogs in one rental unit.

- ✪ Limit the size of dogs by weight.

- ✪ Require that dogs must be spayed or neutered.

- ✪ Require that dogs must be kept securely on a leash and accompanied by the owner/dog walker when outside.

- ✪ Require that all dog solid waste be picked up and properly disposed of.

- ✪ Require that dogs have annual vaccinations, and require proof of vaccinations to be presented to landlord for lease renewal.

Specifically for Those with Cats

- ✪ Require that cats must be kept indoors, or that if cats are outside they be in carriers, strollers, or on harnesses or leashes.

- ✪ Require that cats must be spayed or neutered.

- ✪ Require that the tenant provide one litter box per cat.

✪ Require that cats must not be allowed on balconies or in windows without screens.

✪ Require cats to have annual vaccinations, and require proof of vaccinations to be presented to landlord for lease renewal.

For All Tenants with Pets

✪ Limit pet ownership to particular types, such as dogs, cats, fish, hamsters, and caged birds.

✪ Require that tenants with pets carry insurance to indemnify the landlord in case of damage or injury.

✪ Require prospective tenants to provide references from former property owners and former neighbors.

✪ Require pet owners to provide the name and address of current veterinarian.

✪ Require the tenant to pay for professional steam cleaning of the unit when he or she moves out, stating the cost will come out of the pet security deposit.

✪ Require the tenant to reimburse the landlord for any damage that the animal does over and above the amount of any security deposit.

✪ Require the tenant to resolve complaints from other tenants and to participate and pay for mediation to settle disputes, if necessary.

Landlords should vigorously investigate each complaint about pets that is made by other tenants and guests. Dogs that exhibit vicious natures should be required to pass obedience training, paid for by the dog owner, or be permanently removed from the unit. Landlords should also consider requiring tenants with vicious dogs to carry a certain amount of liability insurance to protect the landlord and property owner from any dog-attack liability.

The regulations for pet owner tenants should be in writing and given to all prospective and current tenants, whether they have a pet or not. Both landlords and tenants should follow these rules.

LANDLORD LIABILITY FOR A TENANT'S PET

One of the reasons that landlords want a no pets clause is the fear that in some circumstances the landlord may be financially responsible for damage or injury caused by a tenant's pet to a third party. Most states are not eager to extend liability beyond the owner of the offensive pet, but it can happen.

Just leasing the premises to a tenant usually is not enough to make the landlord liable. Most courts hold the landlord liable if the landlord: 1) knew the pet was dangerous and could have had the pet removed; and 2) harbored or kept the tenant's pet (i.e., cared for or had control over the pet).

In court it must be proven that the landlord knew the pet was dangerous and had the legal power to make the tenant get rid of the pet. Pets are not presumed to be vicious. However, if a pet was particularly threatening or had caused problems in the past, it may be inferred that the landlord had such knowledge.

As for the power to remove a pet, if the landlord buys a building that has current leases, the landlord may not be able to legally evict the tenant (depending upon the lease and how it handles pets). Harboring or keeping a tenant's pet means having some control over the pet. Some courts have held that if a landlord allows a pet the run of the property without a leash or harness, the landlord does have some control over the animal.

ENFORCING "NO PETS" CLAUSES

Unfortunately many landlords opt to ban all pets instead of doing the modest amount of work required to allow pets. The majority of pre-printed form leases found in stationary stores include a no-pets clause, and a landlord can legally decide to restrict his or her property to no pets. Some cities have restricted the practice of adding a no-pets clause to an existing lease when that clause is added merely to get rid of a current tenant. In that case, the landlord would have to prove that the change was not aimed at a particular tenant and was reasonable for that property.

Another problem with a no-pets lease comes when the landlord has not enforced this restriction. Most courts state that the landlord cannot wait to enforce this provision. If the landlord knows of a pet, he or she must take immediate steps to inform the tenant that the animal violates the terms of the lease and give the tenant time to get rid of the animal. If a landlord knowingly permits an animal to stay for a long period of time, some courts have decided that the landlord loses his or her right to object to that pet. Tenants who can prove to a court that they have been illegally evicted may be able to sue the landlord for the damages suffered as a result.

If a landlord wishes to allow a particular tenant to have a pet, then the landlord should strike the no-pets clause in that particular lease. In no situation should the landlord allow a tenant to sign a lease that contains a no-pets clause if the landlord knows that the tenant intends to have a pet. A landlord who allows this and then sells his or her property may be included in a lawsuit if the new owner wants to enforce this term of the lease.

COMPANION ANIMAL SECURITY DEPOSIT

Landlords who require that tenants with companion animals pay pet deposits must handle those security deposits in the same manner as required by law for other security deposits. The landlord may have separate accounts for the normal security deposit and the companion animal security deposit, just to keep the amounts separated. When the resident moves, if the animal has done no damage to the unit, the deposit will be refunded in the same manner as security deposits are.

RENTING TO TENANTS WITH ANIMALS IN THIS ECONOMY

Many of your tenants are going to be people who have been stripped of everything due to the massive foreclosures and fraudulent mortgages. As a landlord you sit in the seat of power for these people. On their behalf I urge you to let these people keep their pets. That pet may be the only thing that remains of a former happy life.

Many of these pets are older, no longer the cute puppy or kitty that gets adopted. Forcing tenants to turn these loved pets over to a shelter is probably a death sentence for the pet. And the tenant knows this. Showing compassion to these less fortunate animals will earn you the gratitude of the tenants. For the sake of the innocent pets, I urge you to let the tenants keep their pets!

Moving in the Tenants

chapter 24

Being a landlord is not merely knowing the laws and following the rules. There is a large amount of preventative protection that a landlord must do to protect his or her property. This chapter follows the landlord from the point when the tenant is approved to the point when the tenant physically moves in. This chapter also discusses what the landlord or property manager should do just before the new tenant moves in and during the time of the tenant's move in to the rental property.

PROSPECTIVE TENANT IS APPROVED

From the point when the prospective tenant was approved to rent the landlord's property several things should have happened.

1. The tenant should be contacted about the approval and asked when he or she wants to meet with the landlord or property manager to sign the lease. Remember, everyone who is going to live in the rental property must sign the lease. Remind the tenant of that and set a date and time to sign the lease when all parties are available. Do not let anyone begin moving in until the lease is signed.

Right there things can go wrong. The prospective tenant may have decided that he or she no longer wants to rent your property. If you have charged a fee to do a credit check, the law does not require that you return the fee, but sometimes a landlord will do so depending on why the tenant is backing out. Returning the fee is a matter of good will.

2. The landlord should have created the lease to be signed. Other documents that the landlord may want the tenant to sign, such as a garage/parking spot rental agreement, a companion animal agreement, or a storage area rental agreement should also be created. Now they need to be filled in with the correct information for the new tenant.

3. A copy of a full set of rules for the rental property should be provided to the tenant if that has not already been done.

PREPARATION OF THE PROPERTY

Once the landlord has a firm move-in date, the landlord should look at confirming and documenting the condition of the property.

Confirming the Condition of the Rental Property

It is rare for a landlord to not want to keep his or her rental property in the best condition possible, especially regarding issues of safety. For the vast majority of landlords their rental property is more than just a moneymaker, it is a reflection on their work ethic. For landlords who want to participate in HUD Section 8 or public housing programs, their rental property is subject to certain inspections. In addition, some local laws require that rental property be kept up to certain standards and that property can be inspected by the city or town to see if those standards have been met. So, with these things in mind the landlord should do an inspection of each rental property with an eye towards local requirements and safety measures. The best time for such an inspection is before the new tenant moves in as part of an overall walk through.

Landlords know their rental property. They have seen it many times, and maybe even lived in it. The question, then, is how can a landlord objectively look at the rental property and determine if it is ready for tenants. One way is to make a checklist of important items and safety issues for each rental unit.

Here are some of the items that a landlord should check out:

- ✪   There should be no peeling paint either inside or on the exterior of the rental unit. This is especially important for a property that may have lead-based paint.

- ✪   The stove, refrigerator, and dishwasher/disposer must be clean and in working order.

- ✪   The heating and cooling system for the rental property should be in working order with all venting in compliance with local laws.

- ✪   Bathrooms and kitchens should have both hot and cold running water.

- ✪   Toilets, showers, and sinks should be in working order. There should be no plugged or backed up drains. There should be no plumbing leaks.

- ✪   Electrical outlets must have cover plates and be functional.

- ✪   Many states and HUD require that electrical outlets near water be GFI outlets.

- ✪   There should be no broken, cracked, or missing windows. Many states and HUD require working locks on all ground-level windows. Windows that open must have secure screens so no one falls out.

- ✪   Doors to the outside should not be broken, missing, or not functional. All doors to the outside of the rental unit should have locks.

- ✪   There should be no roof leaks.

- ✪   Stairs and railings must not be loose or wobbly.

✪   Floor coverings should not have loose pieces or holes that would cause a person to trip.

Documenting Premises for Security Deposit

The landlord needs to document the condition of the rental property prior to the tenant moving in. That way, if the tenant does damage to the property the landlord will have evidence of what the property looked like before the damage. This evidence can be in the form of digital pictures and a checklist.

Many landlords take several digital pictures of the rental property prior to the tenant moving in. It is much easier to explain to a tenant why the landlord has taken an amount out of the tenant's security deposit when the landlord can show pictures of what the property looked like before this tenant moved in. If this type of case got into a court, these pictures would be considered terrific evidence for the landlord.

Of course, the primary way that most landlords document the condition of the rental property is to use a checklist such as form 06 001, p.275. The best way to use this form is for the landlord to make his or her inspection just prior to the tenant moving in. The landlord notes any damage or wear on specific items. A copy of the document is then provided to the tenant who has the option to: 1) sign off and agree with what the landlord says; 2) disagree with the landlord's evaluation and meet with the landlord about a particular item; and/or 3) request that the landlord fix the deficiencies that both have noted. Feel free to alter this form to meet your needs.

Some landlords present this form to the tenant right after the tenant signs the lease and then accompany the tenant to the rental unit so both parties can together fill out the check-off form. Some landlords merely fill out the form and then leave it in the rental unit. In those cases, if the tenant has an issue with how an item was rated, the tenant can contact the landlord. There is no law governing this procedure.

VIEWING THE TENANTS

Many landlords like to show up when the tenants are moving in. An old trick of experienced landlords is to come with papers (form 08 001, p.283, and form 08 002, p.283) that they need to give the tenant, or with some token gift. In reality they are looking at what is going into the rental property and who is going to live there.

Many landlords have caught tenants moving in items that are not allowed such as water beds, heavy equipment, materials that indicate the tenant wants to run a business out of the residential rental unit, or even drug-making paraphernalia. It is also not unusual for this first visit to find more people living in the unit than are allowed in the lease or companion animals that are not allowed in the lease.

The landlord's response depends on what violation is found. For additional cotenants, a landlord may require that this new person go through the credit check process and sign a lease. For companion animals the landlord may want to have the tenant provide an animal security deposit to handle pet damage. For more important issues such as the tenant wanting to run a business out of a residential property or the tenant attempting to engage in criminal activity, the landlord should point out the rules, the requirements in the lease, and point out that violations can result in evictions.

Four Rules to Follow When Dealing with Tenants

1. Act quickly when tenants cause trouble or do not pay their rent. If you let tenants take advantage of you one time it becomes their normal behavior.

2. Inspect your property regularly. Fix physical problems before they become bigger. Make sure that tenants are not causing damage to your property.

3. Be prepared for problems. Know who you will call to fix plumbing, electrical, or other serious problems. Encourage tenants to let you know about a problem and to not try to fix it themselves.

4. Be good to good tenants. There is nothing better than knowing that your property is in the hands of someone who treats it as his or her own. Once you find a good, responsible tenant, do what you can to keep that tenant.

Section 8

TENANTS—PART 2 THE BAD AND THE UGLY

This section looks at tenants who do things that make a landlord scream. Here we look at some of the most egregious tenant problems, non-tenant renters, tenants who cause problems, and finally ending the tenancy.

A list of problems that a landlord can have with tenants would fill many books. There are, however, some generic issues that a landlord must keep in mind. Your local (city, county, state) laws can provide you with assistance when dealing with problem tenants. In some cities the types of problems that a tenant can cause (such as drug dealing) become an issue where the city steps up to enforce the laws with local police assistance. As a landlord you must be on top of all issues. If you get a complaint about noise, investigate it. If you find a tenant is not following the rules, take steps to enforce the rules. The worst thing a landlord can do with a tenant is to ignore the problems. Ignoring the problems caused by a tenant guarantees that the problems will grow, perhaps to the point where those problems cause your good tenants to leave.

Non-Tenant Renters

This chapter discusses the very sticky issue of people who are not tenants but are living in your rental property. It also provides information on dealing with legitimate tenants who attempt to turn over their lease to another person.

WHO ARE THESE PEOPLE?

Many landlords have had it happen to them. You carefully select the appropriate tenants, you try to be fair and understanding of their problems, and then one day you notice that the two tenants you rented to have multiplied (and we do not mean children). For some unexplainable reason the two adults you rented to are now four or six adults who seem to be coming in and out of the property like they live there. Despite the clause in your lease and the rules that do not allow additional people to live in this property, your tenant has acquired cotenants.

Or you notice that you have not recently seen the two tenants you rented to but the property is occupied, mail is being delivered, and a different car occupies the assigned parking spot. Even though the lease and the rules specifically forbid subletting or assigning the rental property to another without the landlord's permission, you now have a sublet or an assignment.

DEFINITIONS

Cotenant

A cotenant is a renter who has signed the lease and is liable for the full amount of the rental payment should any other cotenant refuse to pay the rent amount.

Sublet

A true sublet is when the tenant re-rents the property to a third party. The third party pays the tenant a rental amount, and the tenant pays the rent specified in the lease to the landlord.

Assignment

With an assignment, the tenant transfers all of his or her rights and obligations for the rental property to another person (assignee). That other person pays the rent to the landlord.

Cosigner

A cosigner is a person who guarantees to pay the debts of another. A cosigner is used when a prospective tenant has poor credit rating, lack of employment, or some other financial issue. See form 11 001, p.282.

WHY THE CONCERN?

The primary reason that a landlord needs to control who can live on the property is one of being able to select a responsible tenant who will pay rent on time and not damage the property.

When a tenant and cotenant sign the lease they are agreeing to be legally liable for the rent and for damages that they cause. All tenants and cotenants are screened so that the landlord can be assured that these people will live up to their liability. All tenants and cotenants must sign the lease document. When a new person attempts to avoid this step by just moving in without the landlord's permission and without signing the lease, that new person avoids much of the legal liability.

In a true sublet where the landlord is left out of the transaction, the subletting tenants are not screened to the qualifications that the landlord has set up. In the majority of these cases the original tenant has moved away and does not have the proximity to see if the subletting tenants lives up to their promises. Legally the original tenant is still 100 percent liable for the property just as if he or she were still living in the rental property. However, that may be of little solace to the landlord if the subletters have damaged the property.

Finally, an assignment is when the original tenant attempts to put another person in his or her place in the rental lease. The landlord may have raised rents, and had the assignee attempted to rent in the proper manner he or she would be paying more to the landlord. As with subletting, if the tenant assigns the lease the original tenant is still 100 percent liable for rental payments and for damages caused by the assignee.

Many of these situations can be addressed by the tenant coming to the landlord and requesting permission for another person move in, for a sublet, or even for an assignment. In that situation the landlord needs to do a standard tenant screening on the new person and should amend the lease (form 11 002, p.288). Many landlords will not amend the lease in these situations but will cancel the old lease and issue a new lease in the name of the new tenant.

ACTIONS THE LANDLORD SHOULD TAKE

Assuming that the lease has prohibitions against adding a cotenant, subletting, or assigning the lease without the permission of the landlord, any hint of this type of activity requires an immediate response from the landlord. The first response can be a friendly, "Who is that additional person?" or "Where is the original tenant?" The landlord may happily find out that the additional person is the tenant's relative who is only staying in town for a month—of course in that case the landlord needs to do a return visit in one month to see if the person is gone. The landlord may hear that the original tenant is off on a month-long cruise and the new people are merely house-sitting for the tenant.

If, however, the new cotenant is a permanent addition the landlord must remind the tenant of the lease. This can be an easy issue to resolve. The landlord makes the new cotenant fill out a screening form, does a credit check, and amends the lease to include this new person.

It may be much tougher for those who are subletting or have been assigned the lease. Here the landlord needs to contact the original tenant. This may be one of those cases where the landlord's attorney should be involved.

PROTECTION IN YOUR LEASE

Most commercial or form leases have some restrictions on a tenant's ability to assign or sublease. These restrictions are usually items like: the landlord must consent to the prospective new tenant; the landlord can reject the prospective new tenant without cause; the prospective new tenant must pass the same screening processing as all other prospective tenants; the tenant may be required to pay a fee, expenses, or an aggregate rent for the re-letting; the new tenant must sign a lease with the landlord that is for the usual length of time for that property rental; the new tenant must pay rent directly to the landlord not the former tenant; and/or the tenant cannot sublet only a portion of the rental unit.

Clauses that restrict assignment or sublease by requiring the approval of the new tenant by the landlord are very common. This approval is based upon the landlord not unreasonably withholding consent. Courts are divided as to what *unreasonable* means. Generally, courts have allowed landlords to refuse consent for a prospective tenant when that prospective tenant does not pass the objective screening process that all prospective tenants must pass.

Outright denial of any assignment or sublease by the tenant is valid under some state laws, but is not always favored by the courts. A few courts have viewed this prohibition as not absolute because it creates an unequal bargaining power between the landlord and the tenant. Some municipal ordinances specifically allow assignments and/or subleases, with certain restrictions.

Waiver

Even if a lease contains a prohibition against subleasing or assignment, if the landlord fails to object to the sublease or assignment in a timely manner then the failure to object in a timely manner may constitute a waiver of the prohibition. Courts have found a waiver in instances where the landlord gave verbal approval even though the lease stated that there had to be written permission; where the landlord assisted the former tenant in obtaining a subtenant by providing "For Rent" sign for the tenant's windows and posted the sublease information on the premises; and when the landlord continued to collect rent directly from the new tenant.

THE TENANT'S LEGAL OBLIGATIONS

Absent specific provisions in a lease or local laws, courts have found that a tenant cannot discharge his or her rent obligation by either a sublease or an assignment. Legally the landlord can pursue a legal action against the former tenant for all damages and lost rent due to a sublet or assignment. It may be difficult to hold the original tenant legally liable if the landlord has approved the new tenant by an objective screening process or by a waiver as addressed above.

A sad fact of life in any court proceeding is that, although the court may issue a binding judgment that says the party is liable for a certain amount, it is up to the person getting that judgment to actually collect on it. Former tenants cannot always be found, their employment and personal references may deny knowing where the person is now, which leaves the landlord holding a paper judgment and nothing else.

The landlord has a few options at this point. He or she may be able to go after the party that the original tenant sublet or assigned to, but they are also probably long gone. The landlord can hire a detective to track the original tenant and, once found, execute the judgment by a wage garnishment or attachment of property. There are law firms that specialize in this type of work. The landlord can sell the judgment to a collection agency and get less than the amount awarded. There are collection agencies that specialize in working with landlords for this very task. These agencies can be found through a professional landlord organization or a search on the Internet.

The Problem Tenant

People are all different. Sometimes what appears to be the nicest tenant turns out to be anything but a nice tenant. Problems tenants come in all forms, from the mildly annoying to those who severely damage the rental property. To deal with a problem tenant who continuously violates the rules a landlord can opt for an eviction. However, for many problem tenants the landlord does not want to invest in a legal eviction, the landlord just wants these people to move on.

LEASE VIOLATIONS

Violations of a lease are viewed legally as either material or nonmaterial noncompliance of the lease contract. Material violations are serious violations, and nonmaterial violations are not as serious.

Non-Material (Less Serious) Violations

Every tenant does something that could be considered a minor violation of the rules of the rental property as mentioned in the lease. The landlord needs to draw an imaginary line around those violations that can cause a run into court for an eviction and those violations that can be corrected with a bit of tenant education.

A landlord may be thrust into the position of being an educator, especially to the "not me" age group that has not been taught responsibility and expects to remain the center of attention as they were in childhood. They can't help it; they were never told that the rules applied to them. Sometimes the landlord needs to reach down and pull up a large amount of patience to help these folks understand that rules like no loud music after 10 p.m. and pick up after your dog need to be followed by everyone. It is a difficult place to be for a landlord who really wants to be kind and give tenants the benefit of the doubt, and at the same time protect the property and keep other tenants happy.

The best place to start is with a friendly visit or letter explaining that the violation was observed or reported, and that it is against the rules or lease (maybe include another copy of the rules), followed by a gentle reminder that rules must be followed. If the violations continue, the contact can go from friendly to less friendly to demanding. While a landlord would love to get rid of the tenant who never picks up the dog poop, it probably is not worth the legal expense to begin an eviction. The landlord needs to remind the tenant that continued violations will mean a non-renewal of the lease or a renewal with a significant rent increase to pay for the additional work that the tenant has caused.

The landlord should keep copies of all correspondence with tenants. That way if a tenant does fight the landlord in court, the landlord can prove the violations of the tenant. This type of evidence is extremely useful when a tenant has reported the landlord to a government agency such as a building code department, HUD, or the EPA and the state law requires that the landlord not retaliate against this tenant by refusing to renew the lease. Evidence of a tenant who has committed several violations could then be presented to the court as a non-retaliatory reason for not renewing or for breaking the lease.

Material (Serious) Violations

Material violations are those items are those listed in the law and lease as being important, or those actions which have severe impact. For material noncompliance, all states require the landlord to deliver a notice to the tenant informing them of the violation. The notice must specify the acts and/or omissions that constitute the breach. The notice also informs the tenant that the rental agreement will terminate upon a date not less than a certain number of days after receipt of the notice (as directed by state law) unless the breach is remedied by the tenant. In all cases, there is a required notice to the tenant and period of time to remedy the violation before the landlord can take further action. See form 15 002, p.295.

In some states the landlord then can recover damages and obtain injunctive relief from the court for any material noncompliance. If the tenant's material noncompliance is willful, some states allow the landlord to recover reasonable attorney's fees for the legal work necessary in terminating the lease and/or obtaining the injunctions.

Common Material Violations

Damages to the Premises

Tenant damage to the premises can be a serious violation or material noncompliance with the lease, especially if it continues after a warning or affects other rental units or common areas that everyone uses. If the landlord considers the damage accidental or something not in control of a good tenant, the landlord may decide to repair the damage, bill the tenant for reimbursement of these repairs, and keep the lease in force (form 15 004, p.296). Another option, if the damage is not serious or will just be repeated after a repair, would be for the landlord to wait until the term of the tenancy is over, then make the repairs using the security deposit for reimbursement.

For an eviction based on this issue the landlord must be able to prove that this problem was caused deliberately by the tenant's failure to maintain the rental unit as required in the lease and in the laws. The landlord should also provide evidence that the tenant was warned and that the landlord attempted to mitigate any additional damage to the property.

Tenant Failure to Pay Rent

Most state laws require that the actual notice for this violation contain the name of the tenant or tenants as listed on the lease, the amount of rent that is due, the location of rental premises, a demand for the rent due, date of notice, and the signature of landlord or property manager (form 15 003, p.296).

A common disclaimer on this type of notice is one that demands that the tenant provide only a full payment of the rent demanded. That deters tenants who try to avoid eviction by providing only a few bucks. The landlord must stand firm on this amount or the eviction notice for failure to pay rent can be invalidated.

That full payment must be spelled out in detail. For example, the lease may state that rent is due on the first of the month, and that after seven days the rent is considered late and late rent is assessed a penalty of $25. In our example the tenant does not pay April's rent. On May 1, the landlord demands full payment of April's rent, the penalty, and May's rent. The landlord must put all this financial detail as to what exactly is full payment in the notice to the tenant.

Landlords who continuously have problems collecting past due rents may want to do an Internet search for collection agencies who work specifically for landlords. Yes, the landlord will not get the entire amount due, as part goes to the collection agency, but even a little is better than nothing.

LANDLORD OPTIONS

The landlord has a few options when dealing with a problem tenant.

Option 1

If a tenant violates the rules even after warnings (form 15 002, p.295, form 15 003, p.296, form 15 004, p.297), the landlord can evict the tenant. Landlords who are not familiar with the legal procedures for eviction in their area will need to hire a professional to do the eviction. This means legal costs. Furthermore, a tenant may decide to retaliate against the landlord by filing a discrimination complaint or dragging out legal proceedings due to some alleged slight done to the tenant. Again, this can be expensive.

Option 2

The landlord can let the tenant decide to leave before the lease is up. If the problem with the tenant is dissatisfaction with the rental property or other tenants (who are following the rules), the landlord may want to make a deal with this tenant. The easiest deal is to let this tenant break the lease and move out without any financial penalties. See form 15 001, p.294. This works with tenants who are unhappy with the rental property and have complained about things that cannot be changed.

Option 3

The landlord can wait until the lease is about to end and notify the tenant that his or her lease will not be renewed. See form 15 005, p.298. However, be warned, many states make it illegal to refuse to renew a rental lease as retaliation against a tenant who reported the landlord to a government agency. If this problem tenant has caused building inspectors, EPA inspectors, or other government inspectors to come to the rental property the landlord must find a legitimate reason (other than being reported to the authorities) to not renew the lease.

IGNORING TENANT VIOLATIONS

If a landlord does not take action against a tenant who violates the lease and/or a local ordinance, some courts have found that the landlord then forfeits the ability to take action against the tenant for this same violation in the future. In these cases the landlord was proven to actually know the violation had taken place, but did nothing, and did not even send a notice of a violation to the tenant.

Are there times when it is better for the landlord to just ignore violations?

The answer is a resounding yes. But it all depends on you, your goals, and what the violations are. If your best tenant, an elderly person, has brought in a caregiver to live in the rental, common kindness on your part dictates that you not demand that the caregiver fill out forms, put down a deposit, etc. If you rent out a house to a great tenant who has always paid rent on time and you know the tenant has just lost his job, you may want to relax the penalties for late rent. In that case you may even allow the tenant to work off some of the rent by doing work on the property.

The best rule of thumb when dealing with tenants is to remember they are people and sometimes the rules need to bend. Evicting a person who cannot pay rent for a few months until he or she gets a new job leaves you with a vacant house and the need to find new tenants. We all need to deal with our fellow man and woman with kindness. As a landlord you have the power to make and to bend the rules out of kindness and concern for others. Having been in this business for a number of years I can assure you that every kindness you offer to another will come back to you.

chapter 27

Ending a Tenancy

All leases come to an end. Sometimes the natural end of a tenancy is a relief for the landlord, who desperately needs to raise the rental charge. A rental property lease can also come to an end prematurely due to a party of the lease violating the terms or other unavoidable matters. Unfortunately there are instances when a landlord must take action to end the tenancy before it comes to its natural end. Usually these involve tenants who break the rules or break the law. Finally there are events in a tenant's life that may cause them to need to get out of a lease. This chapter is a brief discussion of the landlord's action when ending the lease.

LEASE ENDS NATURALLY (GOES TO THE END OF THE TERM)

For the majority of landlords and tenants, a yearly lease will run for one year and a month-to-month lease will be renewed every month. For the yearly lease, the only point where the landlord and the tenant are concerned is a few months prior to the natural end of lease when both sides must decide if they want to renew. See form 15 006, p.299.

As for the procedure to inform the other party about the decision of renew a lease, that can be controlled by the clauses in the lease. One common way to handle renewals in a multi-unit building is to require that tenants who wish to leave at the end of the lease notify the landlord sixty days before the lease ends. That way the landlord has an opportunity to begin the search for replacement tenants.

The sixty-day notification clause can also be expanded to state that tenants who do not provide a sixty-day notice will have their lease automatically renewed for the same term as the prior lease. This renewal would not be at the old rental price but at the rental price which is being charged during the month of renewal. That way even renewing tenants can have their rent increased. Of course, the landlord may want to make some concessions on this for those really good tenants that the landlord wants to retain. In addition to the notification clause, a lease should contain a clause that allows the landlord to raise rents for renewals.

On the landlord side, the lease may require that the landlord notify the tenant sixty days prior to the end of the lease if the lease is going to be renewed and if there is a rent increase. It is only fair that both parties provide the same amount of notice to each other. If the tenant decides not to accept the renewal with the increased rent, the landlord still has sufficient time to begin looking for new tenants.

Some states have laws that control the issue of renewals and the time of notification for a non-renewal. Please check the state and local laws where your rental property is located.

Options to Cancel

A lease can require certain notices or other actions, as long as the lease conforms to both state and local laws. Some leases provide for an option to terminate prior to the expiration date. This option will impose both penalties and requirements on the party exercising the option. This type of option may be applicable to rental properties that are in high demand and/or tenants who are unsure of the amount of time they will remain in the area.

WHEN THE TENANT WANTS OUT

It is not unusual for even a good tenant to need to get out of a lease early. Many times the reasons are legitimate—job transfer, family illness, military duty, or other unavoidable issues. That makes it tough on the landlord. Do you let this tenant break the lease and, if so, what can be done about the lost rental income?

There is no one answer that will work for every situation, but there are some options.

Option 1
The landlord has a legal contract (lease) that requires the tenant to pay rent for a particular length of time. The landlord tells the tenant that he or she can leave but that rent payment must go on. The landlord may even take the tenant to court to enforce the contract.

Option 2
The landlord allows and may even assist the tenant in finding another tenant to sublet the property. This may be as simple as helping the tenant write an ad to go in the local newspaper (tenant pays for ad), and suggesting that the tenant put up notices at grocery stores, at community centers, or at the tenant's workplace. Of course the subletting tenant must be approved by the landlord. It is common for tenants in a multi-unit building to have friends who are anxious to move in. If a subtenant cannot be found, the tenant is legally on the line for the rent until a new tenant moves in. Whether the landlord wants to pursue this in court is, again, a personal issue.

Option 3
The landlord looks at the reason the tenant wants out and, if it is something unavoidable, lets the tenant go. The tenant forfeits his or her security deposit. Landlords who have a popular building or those who list their property through a real estate professional know that they will be able to rent their property with little or no delay. While this may cost the landlord one or two months' rent, sometimes letting the tenant go is really the honorable way to handle the situation. Remember, being able to take someone to court does not mean that you should. Lawsuits are expensive and time-consuming, and if the tenant has no money the landlord is out both the legal expense and the lost rent. See form 15 001, p.294.

WHEN THE LANDLORD WANTS THE TENANT OUT

Evictions   Eviction is the dirty word that both landlords and tenants dread. For the landlord it means more work, following court rules that don't seem to make sense, and having to spend money on a lousy tenant. For the tenant it means the loss of a home, the result of a failed financial venture, and a blot on the tenant's credit history for years to come. It is not unusual for a landlord to begin legal service of eviction against a tenant only to have the tenant launch a major court fight against the landlord. Evictions in today's litigious society are complex and potentially problematic legal procedures that follow a strict set of state and local laws.

Every state and some cities have their own laws regarding evictions. Those laws must be followed to the letter. Generally each eviction begins with a specific notification provided to the tenant. Laws may require that the notice contain specific language, be served in a specific manner, and provide a certain number of days for the tenant to leave. In any type of eviction not following each term of the law can cause the landlord legal problems.

A landlord may encounter any number of common problems when attempting to give notice to the tenant about an eviction. State laws vary, and some require that the landlord serve the notice of eviction to tenant in person or have a process server serve the notice of eviction to the tenant in person. There can be a real problem if the tenant has already moved out. Most states will allow alternate forms of service. This is one reason to keep the tenant's employment information on file. If the tenant is not at the rental property, the landlord may be able to track the person down through his or her employment.

We are currently in a climate where social groups and the courts are heavily concentrating on tenants' rights. If you do an Internet search on "tenants' rights" you are bound to find at least one organization in your town that protects tenants from the nasty, mean landlord. In some of the bigger cities there are many of these organizations helping tenants of every race, creed, color, nationality, religion, and social-economic level. These organizations can have an impact on a landlord who is attempting to evict a tenant. They can marshal media attention, picket the rental property, look for building code violations, send in city inspectors, or pay the legal fees for the tenant to fight the eviction in court.

NOTE: *In many cases where the landlord is attempting to evict a family with small children, especially in winter months, the courts will side with the family. Be aware that evictions of a family with no income and no place to go may cause the judge to grant a temporary halt on the eviction so the family is not put out on the street. This could delay the actual eviction for a period of time or until a local social agency can find the family another place to live. On slow news days this is the type of news story that our twenty-four-hour media loves to broadcast. It is not the best type of publicity for any landlord.*

Self-Help by the Landlord

For years many landlords performed what is called "self-help" in evicting a tenant before the end of the lease without the aid of an attorney. This alleged self-help resulted in unscrupulous landlords who would shut off electricity, discontinue heating the rental unit, change locks, or do other things that would force the tenant out. Unfortunately, in some parts of the country that can still happen. However, that type of action is against the law in almost every state and may result in the landlord paying fines and not being able to proceed with a normal eviction. It may also result in the tenant being able to sue the landlord for damages, court fees, and attorney's fees, or, in the worst case, a discrimination suit. For a proper legal eviction, the landlord must go through the legal process as required under state law.

Currently all states have enacted laws regarding the procedures that must be followed to legally evict a tenant. Landlords who do not follow the laws can be brought into court, charged with a violation of law, fined, required to make financial restitution to the tenant, and given any other punishment the laws allow.

The best solution for a landlord who is considering evictions is to have someone who is experienced in this matter handle the procedure. Some real estate attorneys concentrate on representing landlords in evictions. The landlord may be able to find such an attorney through a local bar association, a local landlord association, or through a real estate professional. If the landlord has hired a property management company to handle the rental property, they probably will be able to also handle evictions.

Why Self-Help Is Not the Answer

As mentioned, some landlords still believe in self-help—locking tenants out, tossing their belongings on the curb—as part of the eviction process. In today's society there is no need for the landlord to stoop down to being a bully. Furthermore, such actions can have long lasting ramifications for the innocent victims of self-help.

I grew up hearing about the landlord who used self-help to evict my mother's parents from their apartment for late rent. For years my mom would talk about being a terrified 4-year-old watching her only piece of furniture, an old cedar chest, hurtling down a flight of stairs, breaking open, and sending all her belongings out on the street. She never forgot the pain and the fear of a child being pushed out of the only home she had known. After my parents passed away I found that old cedar chest, with its broken lid and bent hinge, in my parents' attic. My mom had kept this sad relic to remind her just how bad things could get. To those landlords and property owners who want to hold on to the old ways of physically forcing a tenant out, please think of the red-haired 4-year-old child who carried the scars of that terrifying incident for seventy-two more years.

Mitigation of Damages

Whenever a lease is terminated, whether the termination is because the lease is at its expiration date, because of a tenant's default, because of an assignment, or because of abandonment by the tenant, the landlord must take steps to preserve his or her right to sue for damages. Courts look at the duty of the landlord to mitigate damages as documenting the damage caused by the tenant, and then initiating a repair if leaving the damage unrepaired could increase the extent of the damage and/or the cost to repair.

Example:

Some tenants undertook a chemistry experiment that inadvertently damaged the roof of the rental property. The tenants abandoned the property before the landlord could evict them. The landlord had to document all damage, take pictures, and keep receipts for repair. The landlord also had to mitigate the damage by immediately beginning a repair before more of the rental property was destroyed by the damaged roof.

Surrender or Abandonment

In most formal leases, the word surrender is associated with the tenant returning the keys for the rental property to the landlord at the end of the rental term. There are instances when a tenant may surrender the property other than at the end of the lease, such as when the lease provisions require a surrender, when there is a court ordered surrender, when the tenant exercises a legal option to surrender, or when the landlord and tenant agree to end the lease.

The difference between surrender and abandonment is that in most cases the landlord must assume that the tenant has abandoned the rental property, whereas in a surrender the landlord knows for sure that the tenant has left the rental property because the landlord has agreed to let the tenant out of the lease early. By the landlord agreeing to a surrender, the lease is terminated, as is the tenant's obligation under the lease to pay rent. In some cases, it may be in the landlord's best interest to agree to a surrender just to be rid of the tenant rather than spending the time and money to take the tenant to court.

TENANTS WHO LEAVE WITHOUT NOTICE

Sometimes tenants leave without notice. The landlord is happily going along getting monthly rent checks, the rental property is in good condition, the tenants are happy, and then one month the rent is short or doesn't show up at all. Tenants stop rent payments for a number of reasons—they are repairing the rental property and have deducted the repair from the rent, they have no money but still want to live on the property, or they have run off.

Tenant abandonment is increasing as tenants find themselves unable to pay monthly rent due to job loss, downsizing, or other money problems. If you are renting a multi-unit building in today's economy you will likely have a tenant walk out mid-lease. Legally, a tenant is considered to have abandoned a rental unit when:

- ✪ the tenant notifies the landlord that he or she will not return to the rental unit;

- ✪ the tenant has been absent from the rental unit for a particular period of time;

✪   the tenant has removed his or her personal property from the rental unit; and

✪   the rent is unpaid for a certain period of time.

Because a general abandonment is one where rent is unpaid, the landlord would proceed to terminate the tenancy under a "failure to pay rent" reason. Some states and local municipalities have included ordinances that provide additional detail as to what is a legal abandonment. The common details include: the tenant was absent from the rental unit without paying rent for a period of one rental period; and/or the tenant removed his or her personal property and the landlord is unable to make contact with the tenant.

Many states do not care if the tenant removed his or her property because the abandonment rule rests on a nonpayment of rent and an absent tenant. The landlord may wish to include a provision in the lease for those tenants who may be away from their rental property for long periods of time. This provision would require notice to the landlord and rent prepayment. As with every issue in the landlord/tenant relationship, the landlord must check the laws of the state and city where the rental property is located.

TENANTS WHO DO NOT LEAVE AT THE END OF THE TERM

A common mistake with tenants is thinking that if they do nothing at the end of the lease, then the lease automatically renews itself for the next year at this year's rent. Without such terms being part of the lease or being state law, that is not true. Many times landlords use a lease renewal to increase the rental charge.

Legally the term for a tenant who has received notice from the landlord that the lease will not be renewed and who does not vacate the rental property at the end of a tenancy is "holding over." Most states have laws addressing "holding over after notice" and what to do when a tenant will not deliver possession of the rental premises after notice to quit or at the end of the lease term.

Some common remedies for the landlord are:

- ✪ renew the lease for one year at a significant increase in the rent (if state law allows the rent increase);

- ✪ create what is called a "tenancy at sufferance" with a daily rental rate;

- ✪ create a month-to-month tenancy at increased rent; or

- ✪ begin a legal eviction.

The landlord must follow state law for the approved remedies for a holding over tenant. The key point is that the landlord must issue the tenant a notice—either a non-renewal of the lease notice or a notice that the term of the tenancy is up due to the tenant not paying rent, not following the rules, etc.

Some states will also allow the landlord to file for reimbursement for any amount that the holding over costs the landlord. These would be things like increased cost for renovations that were about to happen to the rental property but due the holding over were delayed, and the loss of rent payment from new tenants who could not wait until the holding over was terminated to move in.

PERSONAL PROPERTY ABANDONED BY THE TENANT

When a tenant abandons the rental property or exits at the specified end of the lease and leaves some personal property behind the landlord may be able to seize that personal property to offset the amount of rent due, again depending on state and local law.

Some state laws cite an old common-law right of the landlord to seize property as "distress for rent" or "distraint for rent." These antiquated terms still show up in real estate laws. Basically they mean a common-law right for the landlord to seize personal property that was abandoned for payment of rent due. In the past some landlords used this law to lock the tenant out of his or her apartment because of back rent owed, but the majority of state laws do not allow that tactic to be used anymore. One reason is that there are better methods to get past-due rent, and locking a family out of its home may injure innocent children. In most instances, the personal property left when a tenant abandons his or her rental unit is probably not worth as much as the rent due, if it is worth anything at all.

SECTION 9

SECURITY DEPOSITS

This section is all about security deposits in the landlord/tenant relationship. Security deposits are of major importance when it comes to a rental. Many cities, counties, and states have laws that direct how security deposits are handled and when they can be returned. We begin with the basics about security deposits, go to how to deal with a security deposit during the tenancy, and end with the return of the security deposit.

Understand Security Deposits

This chapter goes into the complex and confusing issue of security deposits. The issue of security deposits is the third most-litigated issue between landlords and tenants, behind discrimination and eviction. Many of these cases could have been avoided if the landlord and tenant understood security deposits and what they can and cannot be used for.

WHAT IS A SECURITY DEPOSIT—THE LAW

Legally a security deposit is an amount of money given to the landlord by the tenant to assure the landlord that damages to the rental property caused by the tenant will be paid for. Anything beyond the simple issue of using a security deposit to cover the cost of repairing damage done by the tenant is detailed in the local and state laws.

Every state has laws on security deposits.

- ✪ The amount of the security deposit is sometimes shown as a percentage of a monthly rental charge. The most common size of the initial security deposit is a full month's rent.

✪ Many states/cities require that the landlord put the security deposit in an interest-bearing account. Interest can either go to the tenant or be used by the landlord for repairing damages.

✪ Because security deposits are for repairs of damage that the tenant caused, most states require the landlord to provide the tenant with a detailed billing, including copies of invoices for work done.

✪ Generally, security deposits are only for repairing actual damages. Common wear and tear on the rental unit, remodeling, and redecorating by the landlord should not be taken out of the security deposit.

✪ Landlords need to keep detailed records of what the rental unit looked like before and after the tenant. The best type of evidence is digital pictures and copies of invoices from any repairs to the rental unit.

✪ Landlords are also allowed to charge additional security deposits for certain extras such as keeping companion animals, storage of large pieces of equipment or recreational vehicles, or other potential out-of-the-ordinary services that are not listed in the lease.

State and local laws on security deposits can be lengthy and very detailed. In some cities the laws on security deposits are far more extensive than what the state laws are. Federal laws do not go into the same level of detail; their major concern is enforcing the laws of discrimination as those laws apply to security deposits. The charged security deposit must be the same for all tenants.

There are some housing discrimination cases that are based on landlords who charge a particular race higher security deposits than other tenants. This and all types of discrimination are very serious problems and a landlord can spend a huge amount in time and money defending discrimination charges.

When it comes to setting the amount for security deposits, the safest way is to make the security deposit equal to one month's rent.

That works for the landlord who rents out one home and the landlord who rents out various sizes of condominiums. It also works for the landlord who increases the rent for the number of people occupying the property.

For other services such as a companion animal agreement, additional storage, additional parking, or any other service, the landlord can then determine if that additional service warrants a security deposit. For example, it is common to require a security deposit when the tenant has a companion animal on the property. That security deposit is not as much as a month's rent but would reflect a fair amount for cleaning after the tenant has gone. Some landlords charge a deposit for each animal, but that can be problematic when one animal dies.

WHAT'S IN A NAME?

The biggest problem that landlords have with security deposits is that tenants wrongly assume that since the security deposit is the same amount as a monthly rental payment, it can be used as their last month's rent. To make matters worse, landlords routinely say that they need "first and last month's rent, for a security deposit." So let's get it clear: A security deposit is not the last month's rent. It is a deposit set aside for repairing damages.

Most tenants are used to thinking about the security deposit as being the last month's rent. Even the best tenants, who clean up the rental after they leave, fall into that same misconception. If all tenants cleaned up the rental, repaired any damages that they caused, and left the rental in the same condition as when they moved in, it would be easy for the landlord to let this issue of confusion stand. However, not all tenants are so responsible and the landlord must protect his or her property.

Many experienced landlords have used the phrase of first and last month's rent for years. They expect and condone the idea that the tenant will use that security deposit as the last month's rental payment. However, the landlord can get burned when, after the tenant is long gone, the landlord finds out that the rental property has extensive damage and the security deposit has already been applied to the rent.

It doesn't take much damage to cost a lot. A few nasty cigarette burns or stains and the entire room needs new carpeting.

CLEARING UP THE CONFUSION ABOUT SECURITY DEPOSITS

It is up to the landlord to clear up any confusion about what a security deposit is and what it should be used for.

✪   Begin with a conversation about the amount of money the tenant needs to present when signing the lease. The phrase, "We require the first months rent in advance, plus a security deposit of $————," verbally separates the rent from the security deposit.

✪   The landlord should also explain the security deposit to the prospective tenant. This explanation should include the amount of the required deposit, what happens to the deposit while the tenant lives there, whether the security deposit accrues interest and who gets the interest, how damages are determined, how damages are calculated, and any local law regarding security deposits.

✪   The landlord may want to provide the tenant with written information regarding security deposits. This could be a copy of the procedure that the landlord uses in determining damages or a copy of information from the state. (See Appendix A.)

✪   The landlord may want to include a clause in the lease that states that security deposits are used to pay for damages to the rental unit and not for monthly rent.

✪   The landlord should issue a separate receipt for the security deposit. By issuing a separate receipt for this money, the tenant is again reminded that the security deposit is separate from rent.

✪   Finally, about a month or so before the tenant is about to move out, the landlord may want to again remind the tenant of how deductions from the security deposit are made. Many landlords will suggest that the tenant clean the rental unit and repair damages at that point so that his or her entire security deposit is returned. It is not unheard of for the landlord to offer the tenant use of cleaning materials or even a rug cleaning machine.

Again, I know that there are landlords who will say, "What does it hurt to have the tenant use the security deposit as the final month's rent?" To that I say that in the vast majority of cases it does not hurt, but a tenant can leave lots of damage that is expensive to repair, and if the security deposit is used for rent payment the landlord has nothing to pay for these repairs. Very few landlords are so independently wealthy that they can afford to pay for an extensive clean-up/fix-up of a rental unit.

BASICS OF A SECURITY DEPOSIT SYSTEM

Before the first tenant signs a lease the landlord must be sure about the local and state laws regarding security deposits. Go to Appendix A for state law references. For local laws, see if the city where the rental property is located has a website. If not, you may want to call the city and ask where such information is located.

Many states require that a landlord set up a separate bank account to hold the security deposits. Sometimes that requirement is only for buildings with multiple rental units; however, even if you are going to rent out one piece of property it is easier if the security deposit is kept in a separate account. The primary idea of a separate bank account for the security deposit is that you will not commingle security deposits with other funds, like rents paid. By keeping the security deposit separate from everything else it will be easier to pay for damages to the property and to refund what is due the tenant at the end of the tenancy. In practical terms, you should keep the security deposit money separate from any other money because legally the security deposit is not earned money. Also, if all money is dumped in just one account it will be extraordinarily hard to separate the security deposit money from everything else in order to pay all or part of it back to the tenant.

The issue of interest on security deposits is also determined by state law. Some states are silent on this issue; therefore a prudent landlord would want to put the security deposits in an interest-bearing account and keep the interest as a hedge against extreme damages. There are a few cities that actually provide for the amount of interest that such an account will accrue and how much should be returned to the tenant.

Determining Damages

The heart of any security deposit plan is how the landlord determines if the tenant has caused damage to the rental unit and how that damage is paid for out of the security deposit. The landlord must be fair in determining what is damage caused by the tenant and what is normal wear and tear, and the landlord should document the condition of the property before and after this tenant.

One common way to document the condition of the rental unit is to use a check-off form like form 06 001, p.275. The landlord uses this form to make the inspection prior to the tenant moving in. Once this form is filled out the landlord should give a copy to the tenant as part of the tenant move-in procedure.

An additional way to document the condition of the rental unit is for the landlord to take digital pictures of all rooms prior to the tenant moving in and after the tenant moves out. It should be easy to compare what the rental unit looked before and after this tenant.

chapter 29

Changes in the Security Deposit

This chapter covers two common actions regarding security deposits:

1. increases due to other factors/services; and

2. when the property is sold.

It is not unusual for a landlord to need to change the amount of the deposit required for a rental, and we will discuss the various times this is appropriate. Also, the landlord will need to take certain steps with security deposits if the building is sold prior to the end of the rental.

CHANGING THE SECURITY DEPOSIT

A landlord may decide that he or she needs an additional security deposit for a rental. The first thing that the landlord must determine is if the local laws (city, county, state) allow security deposits to be increased. Most cities do not allow any increase until a new lease is signed, which means that the landlord cannot get an additional security deposit until the existing lease runs its term. In these cities the landlord may be able to obtain an addition deposit if it entails a new service for the tenant and a new agreement for this additional service.

An example of this would be a landlord allowing pets to an existing tenant if the tenant signs a pet agreement and puts up an additional pet deposit.

The second thing that the landlord must look at is the existing lease. If the lease specifies instances where the security deposit can be increased and the local law allows this, the landlord may consider raising the security deposit. But be careful, even without a specific law against raising security deposits, courts do not look fondly on the landlord that increases a security deposit in the middle of the lease without providing anything additional to the tenant. Most courts in the United States prefer that the landlord wait until the current lease expires, and then in the new lease an additional security deposit can be required.

Landlords should not change security deposits just because they need more money; there must be some logical tie to the increase. Things like upgrades to the units, upgrades to the common areas, or installation of additional security such as more lighting, dead bolts on all unit doors, or on-premises security guards are logical reasons for an additional charge. Again, make sure that you can legally raise the rate of the security deposit and make sure you handle this addition in the manner prescribed by local laws.

SECURITY DEPOSITS AND SELLING THE PROPERTY

Many times a problem with security deposits arises when the rental building is sold. According to the law in most states, when the landlord sells a rental building the new owner takes possession not only of the physical structure but of the obligations identified in existing rental leases. What is supposed to happen is that the new owner steps into the shoes of the previous landlord. Tenants are notified of a new landlord, but nothing changes until each rental lease runs its term. Then the new owner is in the position to renegotiate the lease or have the tenant leave following all the terms of the lease, including terms regarding the security deposit.

In real life this is not always the case, especially in this foreclosure-driven economy. In a worst case scenario, the new owner finds that the bank account that should have contained the security deposits for all tenants no longer exists. Depending on the sales agreement between the previous and new owner, this can be a criminal matter, or at least the subject of a civil lawsuit. But that does not protect the new owner who is legally liable to the tenants who paid security deposits to handle the security deposits according to the law, which may include paying interest on the tenant's deposited amount.

The owner who cannot pay the mortgage on the rental property may have exhausted all funds including the security deposits. The new owners, who believe they are getting a real deal by purchasing a foreclosure, soon find out that they are responsible for the security deposit funds. Yes, the new owners can legally go after the previous owner for these funds. However, in cases of bankruptcy they will join a group of creditors who may only get pennies on the dollar.

What happens to security deposits when a lender forecloses on a property is also not always in accordance with the law. In many cases the tenants never get their security deposits back. In cities that require these deposits to be put into trusts or accounts that are supervised by a third party, tenants have a better chance of getting their security deposit back.

Right now the only recourse against a landlord who has not returned security deposits in a foreclosure is to file a civil lawsuit. It has yet to be seen if landlords/building owners who take federal assistance money will be required to provide more protection for security deposits. One of the goals of federal assistance is to protect both landlord and tenant.

Security Deposits and the End of the Tenancy

As we discussed, the purpose of a security deposit is to ensure that the rental property can be returned to the condition it was in at the beginning of the rental minus any normal wear and tear. When the tenancy is over the landlord must act quickly to resolve the security deposit issue so that the former tenant's security deposit is handled within the time allowed by law.

STEPS THE LANDLORD SHOULD TAKE

✪ After the tenant moves out the landlord should immediately make a formal inspection of the premises. The landlord should bring the digital pictures of how the premises looked before the rental began, along with the form that was filled out.

✪ All damage should be documented. An easy way to do this is to take new digital pictures from the same viewpoints as those taken prior to the move in. For damage that is hard to see, include a close up view.

✪   For large repairs the landlord will need to contact tradespeople who can submit an estimate that includes what needs to be done and an approximate cost for the entire repair.

✪   For minor repairs that the landlord handles, receipts for supplies used and time spent should be accumulated.

✪   This process should result in a financial document as to what, if any, amount needs to be deducted from the security deposit for this tenant. See form 16 001, p.300.

WARNING: Most states have a very short time limit for landlords to do the above calculations and issue the check for the security deposit to the former tenant. Also, make sure that if your state requires interest on the security deposit that the interest is accurately calculated.

The document that should be presented to the former tenant must show in detail what the landlord paid for labor and supplies to return the rental unit to its former condition. That amount should be subtracted from the security deposit. It is a good idea to include copies of receipts and estimates with this document.

PERSONAL NOTE: I know that throughout this book I continually push the landlord to take digital pictures as evidence of property damage. I also know there are some landlords who either do not want to spend the money on such a camera or feel that such a camera is too technically complex. Let me assure you, the photography industry is now making digital cameras for those of us who have little money and even less technical ability. Many of your local discount stores will have such cameras, as do online retailers such as **www.iqvc.com** and **www.amazon.com.** You can inexpensively and easily get the pictures out of the camera at many drugstores and other stores that provide assistance from people who understand this means of photography. It really is worth the expense and trouble to document tenant damage on a digital picture. It makes court cases much more understandable and winnable.

DEDUCTING DAMAGES AND REPAIRS

A big question for the landlord is what exactly are damages. All states agree that damages are not normal wear and tear on the rental unit. Normal wear and tear is the normal abuse that any living area receives from people. The security deposit is not to be used for eliminating normal wear and tear. All states also agree that security deposits should not be used for rehabilitation or redecorating of the rental unit.

Example:

Tim rents a small home to a family for a period of two years. At the end of the two years, the tenants move into their own home, leaving behind a home that has been lived in. Tim finds some damage—in the bathroom a towel bar has been pulled from the wall, in one bedroom the carpet is heavily stained and smells, the living room carpet has a large water stain under a window, and the kitchen has some damage on the wallpaper.

Tim received the following estimates for the above damage:

1.	Repair towel rack	$ 25.00
2.	Replace carpet in bedroom with carpet of same quality	$300.00
3.	Repair living room carpet	$100.00
4.	Replace section of kitchen wallpaper	$ 50.00
	Total estimate	$475.00

Upon further examination of the living room window, Tim finds that it was not the tenant's negligence of not closing the window that caused the carpet stain. A piece on the outside of the window framing is cracked and when it rains water seeps in. Tim cannot charge the tenant for standard maintenance that Tim, the landlord, is required to do.

1.	Repair towel rack	$ 25.00
2.	Replace carpet in bedroom with carpet of same quality	$300.00
3.	Repair living room carpet	$100.00
4.	Replace section of kitchen wallpaper	$ 50.00
	Total estimate	$475.00
	Less damage in living room	<100.00>
		$375.00

Tim also calculates that bedroom carpet has held the stains due to a disintegration of the carpet padding, which is normal wear and tear. Since he cannot charge the tenant with wear and tear, Tim reduces the amount of damage on the bedroom carpet by $100.

1.	Repair towel rack	$ 25.00
2.	Replace carpet in bedroom with carpet of same quality	$300.00
3.	Repair living room carpet	$100.00
4.	Replace section of kitchen wallpaper	$ 50.00
	Total estimate	$475.00
	Less damage in living room	<100.00>
		$375.00
	Less wear & tear on bedroom	<100.00>
	Total Charged Tenant	$275.00

The total that Tim can charge the tenant's security deposit is $275.00. Tim also cannot charge the tenant if he decides to upgrade the carpeting in the bedroom or re-carpet the entire living room. Those would be considered remodeling. The tenant must only be charged for damage to the rental unit that is beyond normal wear and tear.

DISPUTING THE AMOUNT RETURNED

It is common for a tenant to dispute the amount that he or she receives back from the security deposit. The vast majority of tenants believe they have never damaged a rental unit, have never broken anything owned by the landlord, and are perfect angels when it comes to handling the property of others.

Expect tenants to dispute any charges against their security deposit and have your evidence ready. Taking digital pictures from the same viewpoint before and after the tenant leaves is a great way to show damage, as are up-close shots of damage. It also helps the landlord to obtain estimates from professional tradespeople regarding repairs.

Many tenants will cry to the landlord that the landlord spent too much money to get something repaired. "My friend is in carpentry/electrical/finishing industry and he could have cut you a deal." All states agree that the landlord is under no legal obligation to shop around for a rock-bottom deal to get tenant damage repaired. Had the tenant been so concerned he or she should have contacted that friend and had the repairs made prior to moving out of the rental property. The landlord's only obligation is to follow state and local laws as they are written.

SECTION 10

LANDLORD'S DUTIES AND RIGHTS

This section is about the three primary rights and responsibilities of a landlord: 1) the responsibility for safety; 2) the responsibility for maintenance and repair; and 3) the right of entry into the rental property. These three issues are the basis of many laws and the cause of much litigation. This book presents only an overview of these three concepts. Your state could produce an entire book or more on the laws and litigation for each one of these issues.

chapter 31

Responsibility for Safety

The law holds landlords liable in several areas. This chapter goes over the legal responsibilities that the courts have assigned to the landlord.

GENERAL LEGAL RESPONSIBILITIES

The courts in all states demand that a residential landlord know and comply with the following:

- ✪ state and federal requirements regarding environmental hazards, specifically lead-based paint, mold, toxic fumes, asbestos, and other substances that have been identified as potentially dangerous;

- ✪ laws about required security devices, such as peepholes in front and back doors, sturdy dead bolt locks, outside lobby doors that close and lock automatically, special window latches, and sliding door stops;

- ✪ security laws such as those regarding criminal activity both in and on the exterior of the rental property, laws that require that vacant property be maintained and repaired (including boarding up broken windows and securing entry ways);

✪ laws about safety requirements such as smoke detectors, carbon monoxide detectors, posting emergency evacuation instructions, GFS electrical outlets, and storm shelters;

✪ state and local laws regarding rental property including zoning restrictions on the number of tenants in each unit and laws regarding overcrowding; and

✪ state and federal fair housing and civil rights laws.

ENVIRONMENTAL HAZARDS

Laws on environmental hazards are relatively new in the area of rental housing. Many of these laws originated in inner cities where an abundance of older structures are being rented out to Section 8/HUD tenants. Because a property needs to qualify to be considered Section 8, some of these hazards were discovered by investigations initiated through HUD.

One of the most common issues that landlords may be liable for is lead-based paint. This condition can cause landlord liability when tenant children eat lead-based paint chips that cause medical problems. See form 08 002, p.283. As an aside, chipping lead-based paint can prevent a rental property from being certified for Section 8 housing and may prevent certain government-based funding.

The other problem with lead-based paint is exposure when a rental property is renovated, especially when other tenants continue to reside in attached units during the renovations. Landlords need to check with the NLIC and the EPA prior to starting any renovations on buildings that were built before 1978. The EPA requires that sixty days prior to renovations current tenants be given information regarding lead-based paint dangers. This can usually be handled with a notice regarding the renovations location and date, plus the above-mentioned EPA pamphlet.

Another environmental hazard that the landlord may encounter is asbestos. Like lead-based paint, asbestos can be released in a building that is undergoing renovations. Exposure to asbestos can cause major health problems for those who are exposed to its dust. Regulations issued by the Occupational Safety and Health Administration (OSHA) set very strict standards for testing, maintenance of, and disclosure of asbestos in buildings constructed prior to 1981. Many local communities have added regulations on asbestos through their building code ordinances. For information contact your local OSHA office or look on the Internet at **www.osha.gov**.

Lead-based paint and asbestos are not the only environmental hazards that the landlord needs to be aware of. During renovations, great care should be taken not to nick a gas or electric line. New paint and glue used for carpeting may have toxins that cause tenants with asthma to have a medical emergency. Renovations may also uncover mold, which can send toxic spores into the air.

The landlord, of course, needs to follow the laws regarding environmental hazards. In addition, when renovations are being done the landlord needs to: 1) inform all tenants of the schedule—what work is being done and when; 2) be willing to use no-fumes paint or glue if a tenant requests; and 3) hire only those who have experience with and are licensed to handle hazardous substances.

DANGEROUS CONDITIONS

This topic of dangerous conditions can be divided into two major issues: the element of criminal activity on or around the rental property; and the issue of maintenance (covered in the next chapter).

Many state and local ordinances require certain levels of security, which if not followed may make the landlord liable for these deliberate acts if it can be proven that the landlord was negligent in providing the required security. From a practical standpoint, suits brought against landlords by tenants injured by third-party criminal acts are on the increase. Legal duties requiring the landlord to protect tenants from criminal activity and to protect the neighborhood from criminal tenants are starting to become law in many states.

Landlords must take preventative measures to deter crimes. The landlord's insurance provider, local police, and private security professions can assist a landlord in setting up a workable security plan. There are additional measures that may help limit a landlord's responsibility for crimes committed on his or her property, such as: providing all tenants with education on how to stop crimes and information on crime issues in the neighborhood; maintaining the rental property with an eye toward the elimination of hiding places on the outside of the property, easy access, and areas not well lit; conducting regular inspections on critical items such as security doors and other means of access to the building; and encouraging tenants to report dangerous situations and suspicious activity in and around the building, thus making the tenants a free security force for the landlord.

CRIMINAL ACTIVITY

Drug Dealing by Tenants or Tenant's Guests

This is the most common criminal complaint lodged against tenants. It is not just a tenant problem either. Local, state, and federal drug laws penalize those who knowingly allow drug sales on their property. This can potentially include landlords and property owners. If the landlord has HUD Section 8 housing, the landlord is required by law to stop any criminal activity or risk losing the certification for Section 8 tenants. Besides the potential criminal penalties, this type of activity can lead to other crimes, drive away the good tenants, and lower the value of the entire rental property. Landlords must be vigilant in stopping tenants who deal drugs from the rental unit.

Prevention of drug dealing by tenants begins when the landlord interviews the prospective tenant. Carefully screening potential tenants is a must. Leasing and rental agreements should include a clause that prohibits drug dealing and other criminal acts, and makes violating the clause grounds for immediate eviction. This prohibition should also be part of the rules of the rental property and should be promptly enforced.

Domestic Violence Laws

A few states have passed a new type of law that requires the landlord to provide a minimum of protection for the victims of domestic abuse, sexual violence, and domestic violence. Depending on the state law, a tenant who can prove that he or she is a victim of domestic violence who leaves prior to the end of the lease due to the domestic abuse or violence cannot be sued for the rent owed. The tenant must: 1) be under an imminent threat of domestic or sexual violence (meaning that the violence must have occurred within a number of days); and 2) the tenant who wishes to leave must provide the landlord with a written notice a certain number of days before vacating the premises. If there are remaining tenants in the unit, the lease remains in effect for the written term. If the person vacating the unit was the only tenant, then the lease is considered ended after the written notice.

Other laws are also aimed at protecting victims of domestic violence. For example, a tenant who believes he or she is in imminent danger of suffering domestic or sexual violence and can provide proof by evidence from medical providers, police, a court of law, or statements from a victim's rights organization or another such group can request that the locks on his or her rental unit be changed. The request must be in writing and must provide a copy of the listed proof. The landlord has forty-eight hours to change the locks or, by law, the tenant can have the locks changed. The landlord may charge the tenant a reasonable fee for this change.

Tenant's Injuries
Tenants or invited guests of tenants who are injured by criminal activity on the leased premises may try to legally hold the landlord responsible under a theory of negligence or violation of a law to keep the premises free from criminal activity. Even when local and state laws do not require that the landlord take on extra activities to prevent criminal activity, some courts side with the injured victim.

Example:

A tenant was attacked and injured when entering the common area of the apartment complex where the tenant lived. The tenant sued the landlord, stating that the landlord has a duty to protect tenants from third-party criminal activity in common areas of the building. The tenant alleged that the attacker gained entrance through a security door that was broken for one month. The court found that the landlord does have such a duty to protect tenants.

Example:

An invited guest of a tenant and the tenant were assaulted as they left the rental property on their way to the car. The guest and the tenant sued the landlord under the theory of negligence in maintaining the parking area, including a lack of security for the outside of the building in an obvious crime-ridden area and landlord's failure to implement any procedures or warnings regarding criminal activity. The tenant and guest won.

AVOIDING A LANDLORD'S LIABILITY

It is not unusual for a new landlord to create a lease that waives all of the landlord's obligations and liabilities, including those for damages due to defects in the property. Any landlord who does this is foolish. All states will hold the landlord liable for certain obligations and damages. There is no such thing as waving a legal obligation by merely having the other party sign off, especially in issues of landlord/tenant law.

Maintenance and Repair of the Rental Property

This chapter provides information on the very large issue of a landlord's duty to maintain the rental premises. This issue causes many problems between landlords and tenants and can also be the reason for court cases against landlords.

IMPLIED WARRANTY OF HABITABILITY

The legal concept that the landlord makes a legal "implied warranty of habitability" in every rental is the basis of federal, state, and local laws that require a landlord to maintain and repair the rental property. Basically this places a duty on the landlord to keep the rental property in a condition that meets the standards of state and municipal housing codes, sanitary regulations, and building codes. Some states frame this as the landlord providing the tenant a guarantee that the premises are safe and in the appropriate condition at the time the tenant moves in and throughout the term of the tenancy.

Courts have determined that this is a warranty for the intended use of the rental property. So, if the tenant rents a garage for auto storage, the landlord is guaranteeing that the garage is good for storage but not for the tenant to live in.

Commonly the courts require the landlord to repair those defects that can affect the life and safety of the tenant. The defects must be those of a substantial nature. Courts have used the test of whether the defect rendered the rental property unsafe, unsanitary, or unlivable in the eyes of a reasonable person. These courts have also required that the tenant notify the landlord of such defects and that the landlord be give a reasonable time to make repairs.

Common Areas   In a multi-unit building there are areas that are designated as common areas, places that everyone uses. These are the stairways, lobby, elevators, mail room, laundry room, hallways, dock, garbage area, etc. Under the implied warranty of habitability the landlord must maintain all common areas in a usable condition. Some local and state laws are very specific about what must be done to keep these areas in the proper condition. For example, a common requirement is that the mail area be kept secure so that all U.S. mail can be delivered to the proper party and not be taken by others.

LANDLORDS WHO DO NOT MEET THESE RESPONSIBILITIES

If a landlord does not provide rental property that meets the level of required habitability there are several things that can happen, depending on circumstances and state laws.

- ✪   If the tenant or a third party is injured due to poorly maintained premises or premises that are in disrepair, the injured party can sue the landlord for medical expenses and possibly additional money that the court feels is a punishment for not following the law.

- ✪   The state or city may impose fines which can increase for every day the particular repair is not made. For extreme cases some cities have laws that will let the city tear down a dangerous structure. Some cities may execute eminent domain over the property and take it.

✪   If the landlord has insurance on this property, a lack of maintenance or a failure to make repairs may cause the insurance policy to be void due to the landlord's neglect.

✪   Some states will allow the tenant to make repairs or pay to have them made and then to deduct that amount from the tenant's monthly rental payment. What usually happens in that case is that the tenant does not research who he or she selects to do the work. The worker selected may overcharge the tenant. Because the tenant pays for and oversees the work done, that work may not be done in a way that meets the landlord's requirements. The worker may end up making things easier for that one tenant but not for the landlord. The worst part of this arrangement is that the cash flow of rent payments is interrupted.

Repairs   Every lease should specify the landlord's policy regarding repairs. As stated above, some states allow tenants to make repairs and deduct the amount paid to a worker or for supplies from the monthly rent. Landlords in states that allow this should include a clause in the mortgage that requires tenants to notify the landlord before they do any repairs and that limits how much work the tenant can authorize.

Example:

In a state that allowed tenants to deduct for repairs made, a tenant had problems with leaks that were coming from the roof. The tenant happened to work for a roofing company and decided to authorize the re-roofing of the entire rental property. This allowed the tenant to live in the property rent free for many months. In court the landlord argued that had he known of the tenant's intention the landlord would have gotten several competitive bids from different roofing companies or he may have just had the leak repaired. The court looked at the lease to see if the landlord had set limits on the amount of repairs the tenant could authorize. The court also looked at the difference between the cost of the roofing that the tenant had authorized and the bids of other roofing companies.

What a Tenant Should Do

Tenants should be encouraged to report any maintenance or repair issue (form 13 001, p.290). Those reports should be promptly taken care of. Experienced landlords will say that they have encountered the whining tenant who complains about every crack, every spot of dirt, and runs the landlord ragged. While there will always be fussy tenants, the landlord cannot let one report drop because of the tenant's past actions. There is no way to determine if the report by that tenant is not something that will grow into a major expense if it is not repaired right away.

Example:

The fussy tenant who files many maintenance and repair notices comes in with what appears to be a minor issue. It could be, "When the wind blows I hear sounds like things falling between the walls," or, "When I let a full bathroom sink drain I sometimes hear a couple of drops of water in the wall." The landlord feels that these minor noises are nothing and does not bother to investigate.

Noise #1: The tenant is hearing stucco between the bricks of the chimney falling down. The chimney is falling apart and if allowed to proceed unchecked it may damage the heating unit and cause a backup of toxic fumes the in the building.

Noise #2: The tenant is hearing a problem that grew out of a severely backed-up drain. The drainpipes have a small crack that allows drops of water to fall between the walls when a large amount of water is drained from the sink. If not repaired the crack will widen and may destroy several interior walls.

Landlord's Response to Maintenance Requests

Landlords should be advised that even in cases where the maintenance problem complained of seems trivial, all maintenance problems should be investigated and those investigations should be documented. Tenants who do not get the appropriate response to a request for repair may report the landlord to local officials for building code or health code violations. In such case a landlord may be cited, fined, and required to make repairs by the court. In addition, maintenance defects can cause injuries that the landlord may be liable for. A tenant reimbursement for emergency maintenance done (where the law allows), a quick response by the landlord to maintenance problems, and a janitorial fix to what the tenant is complaining of are all less expensive that a court fight or potential fines from the city.

The landlord can and should require that all problems with the building, even those emergency ones that happen in the middle of the night, be reported to the landlord, property manager, or property management company right away. Many property management companies have twenty-four-hour phone centers that can assist the tenant not only in reporting the problem, but in getting the appropriate trades-person out to make a repair. It is a fact of life that most of the major problems such as loss of electricity, loss of water, and storm damage come outside of the normal nine-to-five business day. The landlord may want to pre-authorize emergency repairs, repairs to those items that if not fixed will cause irreparable harm to the building, and repairs to items that are an immediate threat to the health or safety of the tenants.

For non-emergency repairs, it is always better for the landlord to hire his or her own trades-person who is familiar with the building or to have someone who is on the premises do the repair and maintenance before it gets to a point where the tenant wants to take action. Sometimes what looks like just a minor repair uncovers a major problem. Most landlords have an ongoing relationship with a trades-person who can do the minor repairs with minimal expense and may be able to avoid the major problems by preventative maintenance.

Safety and Maintenance Inspections

Tenants who are injured due to a lack of maintenance on the rental property or due to an inferior repair to the property have the legal standing to sue the landlord. Many tenants do sue landlords over an injury that happened on the rental property, especially in cases where the landlord and the tenant are at odds about another subject such as chronically late rent, tenant damages to the property, or tenants breaking the rules. In the vast majority of court cases, when the tenant sues the landlord due to some injury there is an underlying issue between the landlord and tenant.

As a landlord you need to do everything possible to keep tenant injuries to a minimum, and when injuries do happen, act swiftly to resolve all issues. The first step for the landlord is to obtain adequate insurance.

Insurance

The landlord must carry adequate insurance on his or her rental property. This insurance must first protect the value of the property from damage. As property values increase so should the amount of insurance coverage.

The insurance must protect the landlord's personal property in the case of an injury where the court finds the landlord liable. The landlord should purchase a policy that includes coverage for physical injuries, libel, slander, discrimination, wrongful evictions, and invasion of privacy suffered by tenants and guests. That insurance must also protect the landlord from the rising costs of going to court.

Many of the insurance companies that write this type of insurance will also assist the landlord in assessing the property, provide information on complying with local laws, and help the landlord use insurance to lessen the financial burden if the landlord is found liable. This trend toward an increased level of insurance is causing many landlords to raise their rental rates to compensate for this additional insurance expense.

Landlords should also encourage tenants to carry renters insurance. The renter's policy should cover not only the tenant's property but damage/injuries caused by the tenant to other tenants, guests, and other rental units. A landlord may be able to encourage his or her tenants to obtain renters insurance by providing information on what renters insurance is from his or her insurance agent or broker. Why would a landlord care if the renter has his or her own insurance? Because in case of an incident where the insurance kicks in, this additional policy would protect the renter from losing everything as well as provide some coverage for the landlord and other tenants. The landlord should discuss this with his or her insurance agent/broker, who can provide brochures about renters insurance and information to the tenants.

If tenants still get injured despite your best efforts to keep up with repairs and maintenance, encourage your insurance company to settle the claim. Many insurance companies will fight each and every claim, wasting time, money, and the good will of tenants. It is not unusual in certain states for insurance companies to go into litigation rather than pay minor medical bills for a tenant's injury. There are some insurance companies that have a reputation in legal circles for forcing every claim into court no matter how legitimate the claim is. While that may be great training for the insurance company's lawyers and a windfall for the tenant's lawyer, it is not always in the best interest of the landlord to fight over every nickel and dime.

Tenant's Injuries

In several states the law is that a landlord is not liable for injuries caused by a defective or dangerous condition on premises leased to a tenant and under the tenant's control. There are, however, several exceptions to the rule. A landlord may be liable where: 1) a latent defect exists at the time of the leasing that the landlord should know about; 2) the landlord fraudulently conceals a dangerous condition; 3) the defect causing the hurt amounts to a nuisance; 4) the landlord has stated in the lease that he or she will keep the premises in repair; 5) the landlord violates a law that states the tenant is in the class designated to be protected (disabled); or 6) the landlord voluntarily attempts to fix the condition. The key in these states is to include a clause in the lease that expressly states that the tenants are responsible for "maintaining and keeping the premises in good condition."

Inspections

The second step is to provide procedures for adequate inspections and for handling reports of needed repairs.

To reduce the level of liability from injuries due to maintenance issues, landlords should:

- ✪ detail responsibilities for repairs and maintenance in every lease;

- ✪ encourage tenants to report maintenance problems;

✪   set up a written log for each tenant complaint or request for maintenance;

✪   respond quickly to each complaint or request, and if unable to respond or waiting for a part inform the tenant when the repair or maintenance will be done;

✪   inspect each complaint and maintenance request promptly, documenting the inspection and every repair made;

✪   inspect common areas frequently, maybe every day;

✪   schedule inspections of rental property on a regular basis to keep little problems from growing;

✪   use a written checklist to inspect the entire building on a scheduled basis; and

✪   use a written checklist to inspect a rental unit when it becomes vacant.

TENANT'S ALTERATIONS TO THE PROPERTY

Tenant alterations are common in commercial property but rarely done in residential rentals. The exception being those who are disabled who want to install certain assists in their rental property. The landlord can legally handle this in a number of ways. If the change is something that will add value to the property after this tenant leaves, the landlord should pay for the change. If it is something that detracts from using this property for those not disabled, the landlord can not only insist that the tenant pay for the change but can require that the tenant return the property to the original condition when the tenant leaves. Be careful on this issue as you may run afoul of the Americans with Disabilities Act. See form 13 002, p.291.

Landlord's Right of Entry

The issue of when a landlord can enter a rental property is problematic. Again, state and local laws can affect the issue of right of entry by imposing time constraints.

GENERAL RULES

For all states the rule about a landlord's right of entry is that the landlord has a right of entry to inspect the premises, make repairs, supply necessary or agreed-upon services, show the property to potential tenants, purchasers, or contractors, and in an emergency.

Most of these laws subdivide landlord entry into two groups: 1) entry that has been planed before going into the rental property; and 2) entry that must be done without prior notice. Typically state laws require that:

✪ For a planned entry the landlord must provide the tenant a notice (form 14 001, p.293) within a specified number of hours prior to the entry. Commonly, states require twenty-four or forty-eight hours notice.

✪ Planned entry should be limited to reasonable times, keeping in mind that what is reasonable for certain tenants' work schedules may not be reasonable for all.

✪ All states agree that in the case of an emergency in the rental property the landlord can enter without any prior notice.

✪ All states agree that if the tenant abandons the rental property the landlord can enter without notice.

What is Considered an Emergency?

For an emergency the landlord does not need to provide the tenant with a notice of entry. Most state laws use examples such as fire coming from the rental property or water leaking from the rental property as examples of what is considered an emergency.

However, courts have also included instances where a contractor was working on another part of the building and needed access to the rental property to continue work. Noise or even silence can also generate an emergency. Courts have allowed landlord emergency access where police have been summoned to the rental unit due to screams of abuse or sounds of gunfire. Silence from a rental property can also be an issue, especially if a tenant is living alone. If family or friends call a landlord to check on a missing person, the landlord may need to quickly enter if there's a cause of concern.

What is Considered Permission?

We all know that when we agree to let someone do something we are giving permission. In the world of landlord/tenant law valid permission may be given by implication. For example, when a tenant requests that the landlord repair something in the rental property the tenant is giving permission for entry. Not all states require that the landlord provide a notice of entry to make the repair because when the tenant requested the repair the tenant gave implied permission to enter.

The same may go for inspections that are listed in the lease, if the lease specifies the frequency of the inspections. For those tenants who are signing additional agreements for companion animals, the landlord should include a clause that states the landlord will inspect the rental property for animal damage every thirty days. In the real world of landlords and tenants needing to get along, the landlord is strongly urged to provide the tenant advance notice of these inspections.

Additionally, when a tenant is coming to the end of the tenancy some states find an implied permission to show the rental property to prospective renters in the tenant's notice not to renew the lease or in the landlord's notice not to renew the lease. Another issue is when the entire rental property is being sold and prospective buyers want to enter into the tenant's unit. Courts have interpreted a notice provided to all tenants by the landlord of the intent to sell that includes a statement of a future buyer's inspection as being sufficient and timely notice of entry. As always, state laws differ.

Inspections

So, what are inspections and how do they differ from the landlord wanting to look at the tenant's stuff? Inspections, according to the law, are those things that are done for a legitimate purpose, not necessarily an emergency. An example of a valid inspection can be found in the companion pet agreement that the tenant signs. Most of these agreements include a clause that allows the landlord to inspect for damage done by the animal.

Other common inspections are those done by local officials. Some cities require periodic inspections of rental housing to make sure that landlords are providing requirements such as smoke detectors, carbon monoxide detectors, adequate water, electricity, and other utilities. In addition, some public housing programs require periodic inspections not only of the property but to review information with the tenants. All cities have some type of building and safety department, which has the right to demand inspections. The local fire department may demand an inspection to check for safety. The water department may inspect if the water usage is abnormally high. The cable TV provider and the electric company may also inspect for instances of tampering with the provider's service. All these inspections can be done without notice, unless the state law specifies otherwise.

Tenant's Privacy

Legally, without a good reason a landlord may not enter a rental unit to check up on the tenant. Most tenants are very protective of their privacy, and with the advent of tenant's rights groups on the Internet these tenants will be able to quote chapter and verse the local law on entry. The landlord needs to really know what is considered legal in the state and city where the rental property stands.

The safe advice is that a landlord should not force entry except when there is a true emergency such as a fire or gas leak. If the tenant is unreasonable in denying the landlord access, the landlord may be forced to obtain a court order to legally enter the property. Of course, in the case where the landlord needs to make repairs, the landlord need only provide the tenant with the proper written notice for entry. Whatever the landlord decides to do with a stubborn tenant, it should be done with the utmost professionalism as to not cause hard feelings that can potentially lead to property destruction.

Key Changes

It is not unusual for a tenant to take it upon themselves to have all the locks on the rental property changed and not notify the landlord of the change. Tenants do this for lots of reasons: the tenant wants to keep the landlord out due to some illegal activity or damage; the tenant is concerned with his or her privacy even from the landlord; or the tenant mistakenly provided a copy of the keys to a former lover, partner, or spouse who is now causing problems. The landlord should be both sensitive and firm about this situation.

Begin with the lease. The lease should notify tenants that they cannot change the locks in the rental unit without the permission of the landlord. A landlord may want to use complex locks that must be changed by a professional. In small towns the local locksmith can be advised not to change locks on the building without a purchase order from the landlord. Some landlords use keys and locks that have warnings about duplication on the metal itself.

Under certain circumstances the landlord may want to provide the tenants with a lock change service, especially for those who have given out a key to former lovers or spouses. In this service the landlord picks up part of the expense of changing the locks. In some states this is part of the law regarding domestic abuse protection.

In the rules of the rental property, include a rule against changing locks. The penalty for such a change without the permission of the landlord should be the drilling out of the tenant's lock and replacement with locks provided by the landlord, all at the tenant's expense. Landlord's need to be vigilant about tenants who attempt to bar inspections by the landlord, this may be a sign that the tenant is using the rental property for criminal activity. Many states require that landlords terminate the lease of anyone engaging in criminal activity on the rental property. Some states will actually hold the landlord liable if the landlord allows this type of activity to continue after the landlord should reasonably be aware of the existence of the activity.

Courts have sided with landlords who require access to fulfill their obligation of maintaining and repairing rental property. Some states have enacted laws that seem to bridge the gap between not letting tenants changing the locks and letting tenants do what they want.

Example:
In New York a tenant can add an extra lock, but the owner must get a copy of the key.

SECTION 11

INFORMATION FOR TENANTS AND FINAL THOUGHTS

In this section we want to provide some information for tenants. While what we present is addressed to the tenants, it is also of importance for the landlords. Landlords need to have some parameters of what to expect from their tenants. With those parameters, landlords can compose rules for their own property that are relevant to tenant laws and in accord with what other landlords require.

We end with some final words for our landlords and a few predictions for the future of being a landlord.

For the Tenant

This chapter is a very brief overview of tenant issues. There is not sufficient room in this short chapter to address the needs or wants of every tenant. Besides the space problem, every tenant has his or her own personal needs just as each rental is different. The best advice for every tenant is to act in a responsible manner, follow the law, and be kind.

LETTER TO A TENANT

The following is a copy of a letter that was left for the tenant when the homeowner had to rent out the family home because of financial problems:

My Dear Tenant,

I want to welcome you into my family's home and let you know how pleased I am that you have decided to rent from us. I also want to let you know how special this house and the furnishings in this house are to me. That comfy old couch you are sitting on is the place where my husband proposed to me, the overstuffed green chair in the family room is where my dad used to sit and watch TV, and that big wooden table in the dining room is where my family would sit every night for dinner. If that table could talk you would hear about our successes, the winning home runs, the math tests passed, and a college acceptance. You would also hear the tears of a family as parents and then grandparents passed on and as financial problems hit us.

It is my fondest hope that you and your family make your own great memories in the same place that still holds so many of mine. I ask that you treat this home and its contents with the same respect that I would provide you as a guest in your home. Remember, you are holding my family's memories in your hands.

If you have any concerns or problems please contact me right away, day or night.

Terri

I present this because it very accurately expresses all the extreme emotions that landlords have about renting out their family's home. The tenant who is renting the family's former home needs to keep these emotions in mind in order to understand and deal with the landlord.

THE LEGAL ISSUES OF BEING A TENANT

A tenant's legal rights are protected by the local laws (city, county, state) and the federal laws covering housing. A tenant's legal responsibilities are contained in the lease that the tenant signed and any rules that came with that lease. In Section II of this book we discussed the laws and how to find which laws affect your tenancy.

Other than laws, the tenant is governed by the terms of the lease and the rules of the tenancy. The tenant must get everything in writing including all rules, promises, and the actual lease. Once the tenant signs the lease the tenant is responsible for everything in it, just as the landlord is. Courts will not accept the excuse that the tenant never read the lease to get the tenant out of a lawsuit brought by the landlord. It is the tenant's responsibility to read and to abide by the lease and the rules of the rental agreement.

BEING A GOOD TENANT

Before You Sign the Lease

Being a good tenant starts with finding the right place to rent. Before you start touring available rental units get the facts about the neighborhoods and about your available housing funds. Pre-shop the neighborhood—the stores, the parking, the length of commute to your job, and the night activity. Are there gangs in the area? Will you have the peace and quiet needed to sleep? Once you determine what neighborhood you want to live in, realistically determine what you can spend on housing.

How much money do you really have to spend on your rent? In these hard economic times, experts advise that monthly housing costs should not be more than 26 to 28 percent of your monthly income and that your total monthly debt payments (including credit card payments, loan payments, and housing) should not exceed 36 percent of your monthly income. Remember that your rent may not include all utilities. Telephone service is usually paid for by the tenant, as is renters insurance. Be honest about this. Do not waste your time or a landlord's time by viewing rental units that are not within your budget. Above all, do not sign a rental agreement for a rental unit that is way more expensive than what you can pay.

Looking at a Potential Rental

Once you find a place that you are considering renting, make an appointment to see the property. If you are looking at a large apartment complex you may be able to get by without an appointment, but you still should call in advance to make sure there will be someone to let you in.

Tenants should inspect potential rental units carefully for working water, toilets, appliances, windows, and doors. Check for damage to the unit, and if there is damage make sure it is noted in writing as part of your signed rental agreement. A tenant who accepts a rental unit that has damage may end up losing part of his or her security deposit to pay for repairs he or she did not cause, unless the damage was noted at the time of the rental.

Signing the Rental Agreement

Most landlords will require that you provide certain information before you can sign a lease. Lying about this information can cause the lease to be voided. Be honest and prompt in providing what the landlord requires. Make sure that you get a copy of every document that you sign when you rent the property. Most importantly, read the lease and read the rules.

Paying the Rent

It goes without saying that a tenant must pay the rent and pay it on time. Some landlords charge late-payment fees, which will be listed in your lease. Tenants who have a major problem and cannot pay their rent should contact their landlord. In today's economy it is not unusual for a tenant to lose his or her job and be unable to pay rent. There are some understanding landlords who will work with the tenant when a major financial issue happens. One of the best apartment handyman and caretakers I know began this profession when he lost his accounting job and his landlord let him work off his rent by doing maintenance on the building.

A tenant should avoid an eviction at all costs. Tenants who have a history of evictions due to nonpayment of rent may end up being rejected from renting in locations that they desire.

COMMON TENANT ISSUES

A tenant should follow his or her duties as listed in the rental agreement and the rules provided by the landlord. Tenants who cannot follow these rules are subject to eviction. A tenant who repeatedly causes problems is not only subject to losing the right to rent that unit, he or she may also be liable for civil penalties.

Roommates

One common mistake that tenants make is to take on a roommate without informing the landlord. Before you let another person live with you, you must check with your landlord. Most landlords will require that this roommate become a cotenant and go through the same screening you went through. Also, landlords are legally entitled to set reasonable occupancy limits and an additional roommate may violate this limit. Also, landlords can charge an additional rent and security deposit for roommates who are considered cotenants.

Noise

There is nothing worse than excessive noise from a neighbor, especially when you are trying to sleep. Of course, the questions are what exactly is noise, and when is it excessive. To a parent the sound of children squealing is a joy, to the child-free it is like fingernails on a blackboard. And while cranking up the stereo is usually OK, loud hard rock while the other tenants are trying to sleep is just annoying noise. Noise from other tenants can drive good tenants away from a rental community, leaving behind those who enjoy a nightly battle of the stereo speakers.

So, what can a tenant do? The tenant needs to know what is considered noise, and the first place a tenant should look is in the lease and in the rules of the rental. Most rental agreements contain a clause that gives all tenants the right to quiet enjoyment of the premises and requires that tenants not disturb others. In some cases the noise of neighbors may be against the law, depending on time of day and volume. If the noise is coming from a barking dog, the local animal control ordinances may apply.

There are many solutions to the noise problems, including involving the landlord. If your neighbor's loud stereo is a violation of the rental agreement, the landlord may be able to threaten the noisy neighbors with eviction. Sometimes a quiet talk with a neighbor may resolve the problem, but face-to-face confrontations can also result in many other problems. Sometimes reporting a loud party or constantly barking dog to the proper authorities may result in quiet. However, irresponsible neighbors may simply resort to their noisy ways once the authorities have left the area. Tenants and landlords have also resorted to professional mediation in order to curb noise from neighbors. There is no one way to resolve the noise problem.

Tenants who are bothered with noise may need to look inward for a solution. There is a certain level of noise that will happen in any multi-family building. A late-night flushing toilet, an early morning shower, or creaking floors in older buildings are all noises that should be expected. Also, tenants who work odd shifts and sleep during the day should not expect the other tenants to keep quiet during the daytime. Earplugs, sound machines, or other audio distractions may be of help in dealing with noisy neighbors.

Pets I cannot say this enough: Tenants with pets need not abandon their pets in order to get a rental unit. No one should abandon his or her loyal pet companions in order to rent property. It is mean, cruel, and totally unnecessary. There are an increasing number of landlords and property owners who are willing to rent to responsible tenants with pets. Local humane societies sometimes have listings of rental communities that allow pets. Landlords may advertise that pets are allowed. That said, those with pets need to give themselves additional time to find accommodating landlords. In many areas that are hard hit with the horrid economy there are humane societies, veterinarians, and concerned citizens who are willing to take in a dog or cat until a tenant can find a place that will accept pets.

A responsible tenant with pets should provide a potential landlord with proof that the pet is well behaved and has proper medical care. Certificates of puppy training, a letter from your veterinarian stating that the animal is current on vaccinations, and a letter from a current landlord may help. Also, the prospective tenant should offer to pay an additional security deposit for the pet.

Once you convince a landlord to allow your pet, get it in writing. If you are an existing tenant or a new tenant, make sure that you and the landlord sign a pet addendum to the rental agreement. The reason to do this is simple. If the rental community is considered "no pets" but your landlord allows you to keep a pet, that personal favor may be forgotten if the landlord no longer works at that rental community.

An interesting Internet site for those renting with pets is **www.rent withpets.org.**

DISPUTES

It is inevitable that landlords and tenants will disagree. Disagreements and disputes need to be resolved quickly and fairly for both parties. The best way to avoid disagreements with your landlord is to know what is required of both you and the landlord in the lease, the rules of the property, and the local law. Arguing with a landlord about paying for or repairing something that is listed in the lease as the tenant's responsibility is a waste of time and will probably result in hard feelings. Also, a tenant with a history of not causing trouble and being responsible has a better chance of getting what he or she wants than a tenant who has been a problem to the landlord.

Tenants who have severe problems with the landlord or property owners should first try to work out the differences without the assistance of attorneys. People are more apt to negotiate a problem without the perceived threat of litigation that an attorney brings. Tenants should document problems, keep copies of communication between the tenant and landlord, and keep all communication civil. If the dispute does end up in court, a knowledgeable tenant who can prove that he or she did everything possible to resolve the problem in a businesslike manner will go far in convincing the court to listen to his or her side.

Reporting Problems

Items that need repair should always be reported to the landlord as soon as the tenant notices. If a tenant has problems getting these repairs, he or she should inform the landlord in writing about the problem. Landlords who are not prompt in repairs may be pushed by certified letters regarding such repairs.

More severe problems, those that make the rental unit uninhabitable such as no heat or water should be handled more urgently. These types of problems need to be brought to the attention of the landlord immediately and perhaps to the municipality. Landlords who do not respond with repairs may be liable for building code violations, fines, and suits by tenants.

In some cities the law allows a tenant to pay for a repair and then to deduct that amount from future rent. Be very, very sure that your city allows this and that your lease allows it. Even if it is allowed, there are usually other steps that the tenant must follow. Common requirements are notification of the landlord before making the repair, getting a certain number of estimates, and allowing the landlord a set number of days to make the repair him or herself before the tenant takes action. As with everything else in a landlord/tenant relationship, look to the lease and the rules first before you spend money on a repair that you may not be reimbursed for.

Tenants also have questions about making physical changes to their rental. These changes may be due to a tenant's disability or medical problems. While each state has its own laws about this, the federal Americans with Disabilities Act can assist the tenant. Before the tenant makes any permanent modification of the rental premises, he or she must speak with the landlord. The tenant should provide medical documentation for this request and a detailed explanation of exactly what the tenant wants done. Landlords are required to make certain modifications, but not all. The tenant may be well advised to hire an attorney experienced in this type of work to be his or her advocate in this type of a situation.

Tenant's Help Organizations

The Internet has a huge number of local and national organizations that are in business to help tenants. This help ranges from totally free information posted on the Internet to the law firms who advertise that they represent tenants in court.

Besides the huge amount of Internet tenant assistance groups, there is tenant legal assistance through legal clinics, bar association referrals, and law school clinics. Tenants can also find help from local community organizations, local churches, and local political groups.

In addition to the Internet sites that have been mentioned in this book, those living in federally assisted housing can find information and what to do about housing discrimination at www.hud.gov.

Insurance

For a tenant, renters insurance is a must. Many rental agreements will hold a tenant liable if they cause major damage to the rental building, even if the cause was an accident. A fire caused by a forgotten pot left on the stove can result in major damage, and the landlord may be able to hold the tenant financially liable. Additionally, a tenant's property is probably not covered by the landlord's insurance. A tenant can lose everything due to a fire, theft, or natural disaster. Rental insurance is relatively low-cost and can be obtained from those who sell other types of insurance.

Last Words

I hope that the readers of this book find it useful in their adventure of being a landlord. Because this book is addressed to the entire country I have not gotten as specific as I have in previous publications. However, I have provided you with the tools to do your own local research both in person and on the Internet. Use these tools to find out the specifics that relate to your area of the country.

As a landlord you should keep up with the real estate industry to be on top of any legal changes. I have found that the best source of information on any real estate topic is your local newspaper and the newspaper of the closest big city. Yes, newspapers, not the Internet, especially those newspapers that report local house sales indicative of local trends in real estate. Because real estate can be different from one town to the next it is these local trends that will ultimately be of importance to you. While major trends that you spot in papers like the *Wall Street Journal* may eventually trickle down to your area, it is local trends that you need to know about. If you are interested in the housing industry as a whole, the very best publication for all business information remains the *Wall Street Journal*, bar none. I personally read the *Wall Street Journal*, two Chicago papers, and my local paper every day to keep up with business.

I hope that for the first-time landlords who have been pushed into this position by the economy this book provides you with assurances that being a landlord is not difficult and is definitely worth it if that means you will save your family's home. I wanted to provide first-time landlords with all the important tools that I did not have when my parents passed on and I was left with their home. Unfortunately, finances stopped me from renting my family's home out and I was forced to sell it. Fifteen years later I still regret not taking the chance to be a landlord for my family's home.

CRYSTAL BALL PREDICTIONS

One of my dear clients gave me a crystal ball because I would often complain that I could not make predictions. No, it doesn't work. The predictions listed below are based on observing the real estate market for several decades.

- ✪ The housing market will continue on its correction for several more years. When the correction has ended our property will be valued lower than it was during the real estate boom, which topped out 2007–2008. That will hurt those who bought property during that time and those with 100% mortgages or whose property was appraised at a higher than value price to support jumbo mortgages.

- ✪ We know, because the real estate industry is still cyclical, that this buyers' market will eventually go back to being a sellers' market. However, it looks as though, unlike previous cycle changes that were very fast, the move into a sellers' market will be very slow. In fact, some experts are saying that we will not go back to that very hot sellers' market for at least a decade.

- ✪ Mortgage money will continue to be tight. By *tight* I mean that the lending industry will return to the rigorous requirements of the pre-boom era:

  - ✪ The property will need to legitimately appraise for more than the amount of the mortgage.

✪ The borrower will be required to legally prove that he or she has a sufficient income to make the mortgage payments plus an amount to live on.

✪ The borrower will be required to make a significant down-payment. Right now the number looks to be about 20 percent.

✪ Borrowers will be encouraged to use government funding such as FHA loans and the VA loan guarantee.

✪ The result of the above will be a more stable real estate industry that will be much more supportive of renting as a way of living and will no longer scream that the a person must buy a home. The attitudes towards landlords will swing in a more positive manner as renting is shown as the value it really is.

✪ Multi-unit buildings and condominiums are still looking like a worse investment than the single family home. Therefore, more of these will remain unsold on the market. Landlords renting out condominiums and apartments should expect that there will be plenty of competition for tenants.

✪ For landlords renting out their family home, the "rent with an option to buy" is going to become a very common way to sell and to get rental money.

Remember, being a landlord can be a very rewarding job that will keep you on your toes and help you out financially. Good luck to you and all my readers, landlords or not.

Landlord-Tenant Legal Information by State

Housing and Urban Development (HUD)

Listing of laws and other Federal information by state:
http://www.hud.gov/renting/tenantrights.cfm

Alabama

Alabama Uniform Landlord Tenant Act

Sections 35-9-1 to -100 of the Alabama Code
http://ali.state.al.us/legislation/landlord_tenant.pdf

Alaska

Alaska Real Estate Commission

550 W. 7th Avenue, Suite 1500

Anchorage, AK 99501
http://www.dced.state.ak.us/occ/pub/landlord.pdf

The Alaska Landlord and Tenant Act

Title 34.03.010 to .380
http://www.state.ak.us/courts/

Arizona

Arizona Department of Housing:
http://www.housingaz.com

"The Rights and Obligations of Landlords"
http://www.supreme.state.az.us/info/brochures/landlord
.htm#Landlords

Arizona Residential Landlord and Tenant Act
A.R.S. Title 33, Chapter 10
http://www.azsos.gov/public_services/Publications/Residential_
Landlord_Tenant_Act/

Arizona Revised Statutes Ann. §§ 12-1171 to -1183 (Forcible Entry
and Detainer)
http://www.azleg.gov/ArizonaRevisedStatutes.asp?Title=12

Arizona Revised Statutes Ann. §§ 33-1301 to -1381 (Arizona Residential
Landlord and Tenant Act), -301 to -381(Landlord and Tenant)
http://www.azleg.gov/ArizonaRevisedStatutes.asp?Title=33

Arkansas
Landlord/Tenant General Provisions and Tenant Liability: Title
18 (Property), Chapter 16; or Arkansas Code Ann. §§ 18-16-101 to
-306, -501 to -508
http://www.arkleg.state.ar.us/SearchCenter/Pages/ArkansasCode
SearchResultPage.aspx

State of Arkansas
http://www.state.ar.us

Arkansas Attorney General
http://ag.arkansas.gov/consumers_consumer_tips_landlord_tenant
.html

California
California Department of Consumer Affairs
http://www.dca.ca.gov/publications/landlordbook/index.shtml

California Department of Housing:
http://www.hcd.ca.gov

Judicial Council of California
http://www.courtinfo.ca.gov/selfhelp/other/landten.htm

Laws of individual cities in California
   http://igs.berkeley.edu/library/calcodes.html

Connecticut
Connecticut General Statutes Ann. §§ 47a-1 to -74 (Landlord and Tenant)
   http://www.cga.ct.gov/2005/pub/Title47a.htm

Connecticut Judicial Branch–Law Library
   http://www.jud.ct.gov/lawlib/law/landlord.htm

Colorado
Boulder "Landlord-Tenant Handbook"
   http://www.ci.boulder.co.us/index.php?option=com_content&task=
      view&id=3767&Itemid=1406

Colorado Department of Housing
   http://dola.colorado.gov/cdh/index.html

Colorado Revised Statutes §§ 38-12-101 to -104 (Security Deposits), -301 to -302 (Local Control of Rents Prohibited); §§ 13-40-101 to -123 (Forcible Entry and Detainer)
   http://www.michie.com/colorado

Delaware
Delaware Code Ann. Title 25, §§ 5101 to 5907 (Property); Chapters 53 (Landlord Obligations and Tenant Remedies), 55 (Tenant Obligations and Landlord Remedies), 57 (Summary Possession), 59 (Tenant's Receivership), 61 (Commercial Leases), 63 (Distress for Rent), and 65 (Miscellaneous Provisions)
   http://delcode.delaware.gov/title25/index.shtml#TopOfPage

Florida
Florida Ann. Statutes §§ 83.40 to .682 (Residential Tenancies)
   http://www.flsenate.gov/Statutes/index.cfm?App_mode=Display_
      Statute&URL=Ch0083/titl0083.htm&StatuteYear=2002&
      Title=%2D%3E2002%2D%3EChapter%2083

Florida Bar Association
   http://www.floridabar.org/tfb/TFBConsum.nsf/0a92a6dc28e76ae
      58525700a005d0d53/e21a25a8c288bed98525740800537588?
      OpenDocument

Eviction information from Pasco County Clerk of the Court
   http://www.pascoclerk.com/public-courts-landlord-tenant.asp

Florida Division of Consumer Services
   http://www.800helpfla.com/landlord_text.html

Georgia
FAQs from the Department of Community Affairs
   http://www.dca.state.ga.us/housing/HousingDevelopment/programs/
      downloads/landlord/contents.html

Georgia Code Ann. §§ 44-7-1 to -81 (Landlord and Tenant)
   http://www.lexis-nexis.com/hottopics/gacode/default.asp

Hawaii
Department of Commerce and Consumer Affairs
   http://hawaii.gov/dcca/areas/ocp/landlord_tenant/

Hawaii Revised Statutes §§ 521-1 to -78 (Residential Landlord-Tenant
Code)
   http://hawaii.gov/dcca/areas/ocp/main/hrs/lt_code

Idaho
Attorney General's Landlord and Tenant Guidelines
   http://www2.state.id.us/ag/consumer/manuals/LandlordTenant.pdf

Idaho Code §§ 6-201 to -324
   http://www3.state.id.us/idstat/TOC/06FTOC.html

Idaho Code §§ 55-208 to -308
   http://www3.state.id.us/idstat/TOC/55FTOC.html

Idaho Supreme Court
   http://www.courtselfhelp.idaho.gov/landlord.asp

Illinois

735 Illinois Compiled Statutes §§ 5/9-201 to 321 (Recovery of Rent)
   http://www.ilga.gov/legislation/ilcs/ilcs2.asp?ChapterID=56

765 Illinois Compiled Statutes §§ 705/0.01 to 742/30 (Landlord and Tenant)
   http://www.ilga.gov/legislation/ilcs/ilcs2.asp?ChapterID=62

Eviction Notices by Illinois Legal Aid
   http://www.illinoislegalaid.org/index.cfm?fuseaction=home.dsp_
      Content&contentID=854

Landlord & Tenant Ordinance for the City of Evanston
   http://www.cityofevanston.org/departments/humanrelations/
      landlord.shtml

Landlord-Tenant Disputes for the City of Oak Park
   http://www.oak-park.us/Community_Services/Landlord_Tenant_
      Disputes.html

Municipal Code of Chicago: Residential Landlords and Tenants
   http://www.chicityclerk.com/tenantsVRSlandlords.php

Indiana

Indiana Code Annotated §§ 32-31-1-1 to -8-6 (Landlord-Tenant Relations)
   http://www.in.gov/legislative/ic/code/title32/ar31/

Iowa

Iowa Code Ann. §§ 562A.1 to .36 (Uniform Residential Landlord and Tenant Law)
   http://coolice.legis.state.ia.us/Cool-ICE/default.asp?category=billinfo&
      service=IowaCode

Iowa State Bar Association
   http://www.iowabar.org/Public%20Information%20Brochures.nsf/d
      7ff6dc91c517cdb862567ba00690c91/90e709d146d2efb486256e
      e10058acfb!OpenDocument

Dubuque County Sheriff's Department (Evictions)
http://www.dubuquecounty.org/Sheriff/Evictions/tabid/129/
Default.aspx

Fair Housing in Iowa
http://www.cedar-rapids.org/civilrights/fair_housing.asp

Kansas
Attorney General's Tips for Tenants & Landlords
http://www.ksag.org/files/shared/LandlordsandTenants.pdf

Kansas Statutes Ann. §§ 58-2501 to -2573 (Landlords and Tenants)
http://www.kslegislature.org/legsrv-statutes/getStatute.do

Kentucky
Kentucky Revised Statutes Ann. §§ 383.010 to .715 (Landlord and
Tenant)
http://www.lrc.state.ky.us/krs/383-00/CHAPTER.HTM

Cornell University Law School
http://topics.law.cornell.edu/wex/Landlord-tenant

Louisiana
Louisiana Revised Statutes Ann. §§ 9:3251 to -:3261; Louisiana Civil
Code Ann. Article 2668 to 2729
http://www.legis.state.la.us/lss/tsrssearch.htm

Tulane University Law School
http://www.law.tulane.edu/tlsOrgs/tulap/index.aspx?id=4904

Maine
Maine Revised Statutes Ann. Title14, §§ 6001 to 6046 (Rental Property)
http://www.mainelegislature.org/legis/statutes/14/title14ch0sec0.html

Attorney General on Consumer Rights
http://www.maine.gov/tools/whatsnew/index.php?topic=AGOffice_
Consumer_Law_Guide&v=article&id=27933

Attorney General's Model Landlord-Tenant Lease
http://maine.gov/tools/whatsnew/index.php?topic=AGOffice_Consumer_Law_Guide&id=27935&v=article

Maryland

Maryland Code Ann. §§ 8-101 to -604 (Real Property)
http://michie.lexisnexis.com/maryland/lpext.dll?f=templates&fn=main-h.htm&cp

Maryland State Law Library
http://www.peoples-law.org/housing/ltenant/llt.html

Maryland Attorney General
http://www.oag.state.md.us/Consumer/landlords.htm

Department of Housing and Consumer Affairs for Montgomery County
http://www.montgomerycountymd.gov/dhctmpl.asp?url=/content/DHCA/housing/landload_T/landload_t.asp

Information from the City of Gaithersburg
http://www.gaithersburgmd.gov/documents/guide_landlord_tenant_relations.pdf

Massachusetts

Massachusetts General Laws Ann. Chapter 186 §§ 1 to 22 ()
http://www.lawlib.state.ma.us/subject/about/landlord.html

Department of Consumer Affairs and Business Regulations
http://www.mass.gov/?pageID=ocasubtopic&L=4&L0=Home&L1=Consumer&L2=Housing+Information&L3=Tenant+%26+Landlord&sid=Eoca

Michigan

"Tenants and Landlords: A Practical Guide" from State of Michigan
http://www.legislature.mi.gov/documents/publications/tenant-landlord.pdf

Michigan Compiled Laws §§ 554.131 to .20, .601 to .641 (Landlord-Tenant Act)

http://www.legislature.mi.gov/(S(d1cs5a45runrki55pjgx4dmr))/
mileg.aspx?page=getobject&objectname=mcl-Act-348-of-1972

Minnesota
Attorney General

http://www.ag.state.mn.us/Consumer/housing/lt/default.asp

Minnesota Statutes Ann. §§ 504B.001 to .471; Minnesota Statutes § 504B.181, subd. 2(b) (2003)

https://www.revisor.leg.state.mn.us/statutes/?id=504B.001

Mississippi
Mississippi Code Ann. §§ 89-7-1 to -8-27

http://www.mscode.com/free/statutes/89/007/index.htm

Missouri
Attorney General on Landlord-Tenant Law

http://ago.mo.gov/publications/landlordtenant.pdf

Missouri Revised Statutes §§ 441.005 to .880 (Landlord and Tenant)

http://www.moga.mo.gov/statutes/c441.htm

Missouri Revised Statutes §§ 535.150 to .300 (Landlord-Tenant Actions)

http://www.moga.mo.gov/statutes/c535.htm

Montana
Montana Code Ann. §§ 70-24-101 to -26-110

http://data.opi.mt.gov/bills/MCA_toc/70_24.htm

Nebraska
Legal Aid of Nebraska

http://www.nebls.com/landlord_tenant.htm

Nebraska Revised Statutes §§ 76 -1401 to -1449

http://www.legislature.ne.gov/laws/browse-chapters.php?chapter=76

Nevada

Nevada Revised Statutes Ann. §§ 118A.010 to .520; 40.215 to .280
  http://www.leg.state.nv.us/NRS/NRS-118A.html

Supreme Court of Nevada Law Library
  http://lawlibrary.nvsupremecourt.us/forms/standardizedMobile-
    Homeforms.php

New Hampshire

New Hampshire Revised Statutes Ann. §§ 540:1 (Actions against
Tenants)
  http://www.gencourt.state.nh.us/rsa/html/NHTOC/NHTOC-LV-
    540.htm

New Hampshire Revised Statutes Ann. §§ 540-A:1 to 8 (Prohibited
Practices and Security Deposits)
  http://www.gencourt.state.nh.us/rsa/html/NHTOC/NHTOC-LV-
    540-A.htm

New Hampshire Revised Statutes Ann. §§ 540-B (Rental of Shared
Facilities)
  http://www.gencourt.state.nh.us/rsa/html/NHTOC/NHTOC-LV-
    540-B.htm

New Hampshire Revised Statutes Ann. §§ 540-C (Vacation or
Recreational Rental Units)
  http://www.gencourt.state.nh.us/rsa/html/NHTOC/NHTOC-LV-
    540-C.htm

New Jersey

"Tenants' Rights in New Jersey" by Legal Services
  http://www.lsnjlaw.org/english/placeilive/irentmyhome/tenantsrights/
    index.cfm

New Jersey Statutes Ann. §§ 46:8-1 to -50; 2A:42-1 to 42-96
  http://www.njleg.state.nj.us/

New Jersey Courts
  http://www.judiciary.state.nj.us/civil/civ-04.htm

New Mexico
New Mexico Statutes Ann. §§ 47-8-1 to -51
  http://www.conwaygreene.com/nmsu/lpext.dll?f=templates&fn=
    main-h.htm&2.0

City of Las Cruces on Landlord-Tenant Laws
  http://www.las-cruces.org/PDFs/07landTenantBrochureEnglish.pdf
  http://www.las-cruces.org/PDFs/07landTenantBrochureSpanish.pdf

Attorney General: Renter's Guide
  http://www.nmag.gov/office/student/renting.aspx

New York
New York Real Property Law §§ 220 to 238

Real Property Acts §§ 701 to 853

Multiple Dwelling Law

Multiple Res. Law

General Obligation Law §§ 7-103 to -108
  http://public.leginfo.state.ny.us/menugetf.cgi?COMMONQUERY=
    LAWS

Attorney General: Tenants' Rights Guide
  http://www.oag.state.ny.us/bureaus/real_estate_finance/pdfs/tenants_
    rights_guide.pdf

"How to Prepare for a Landlord-Tenant Trial"
  http://www.nycourts.gov/publications/L&TPamphlet.pdf

North Carolina
North Carolina General Statutes §§ 42-1 to -14.2; 42-25.6 to -76
  http://www.ncga.state.nc.us/enactedlegislation/statutes/html/
    bychapter/chapter_42.html

North Carolina Bar Association
  http://www.ncbar.org/public/publications/pamphlets/landlordsAnd
    Tenants.pdf

North Dakota

North Dakota Cent. Code §§ 47-16-01 to -41 (Leasing of Rental Property)
  http://www.legis.nd.gov/cencode/t47c16.pdf

North Dakota Apartment Association
  http://www.ndaa.net/rights.htm

City of Fargo: Disputes between Landlords and Tenants
  http://www.ci.fargo.nd.us/Residential/Housing/Renting/Landlord-
    TenantConcerns/

Ohio

Ohio Revised Code Ann. §§ 5321.01 to .19
  http://codes.ohio.gov/orc/5321

Oklahoma

Oklahoma Statutes Ann. Title 41, §§ 101 to 136
  http://www.oscn.net/applications/oscn/Index.asp?ftdb=STOKST
    41&level=1

State of Oklahoma on Landlord-Tenant Laws
  http://www.ok.gov/OREC/documents/Landlord%20and%20
    Tenant%20Act%20Update.pdf

Oklahoma Bar Association
  http://www.okbar.org/public/brochures/landbroc.htm

Oregon

Oregon Revised Statutes §§ 90.100 to 91.225
  http://www.leg.state.or.us/ors/090.html

Pennsylvania

68 Pennsylvania Cons. Statutes Ann. §§ 250.101 to .510-B, §§ 399.1
to .18
  http://www.attorneygeneral.gov/uploadedFiles/Consumers/land
    lord_tenant_act.pdf

Rhode Island

Rhode Island General Laws §§ 34-18-1 to -57
  http://www.rilin.state.ri.us/Statutes/TITLE34/34-18/INDEX.HTM

The Rhode Island Landlord-Tenant Handbook
http://www.hrc.ri.gov/documents/2007%20Revision%20of%20L_T_
Handbook2.pdf

South Carolina
South Carolina Code Ann. §§ 27-40-10 to -940
http://www.scstatehouse.gov/code/t27c040.htm

South Carolina Appleseed Legal Justice Center
http://www.scjustice.org/Brochures%20for%20Web%202009/Housing/
Landlord-Tenant%20Law%202009.pdf

South Dakota
South Dakota Codified Laws Ann. §§ 43-32-1 to -30
http://legis.state.sd.us/statutes/DisplayStatute.aspx?Type=Statute
&Statute=43-32

Tennessee
Tennessee Code Ann. §§ 66-28-101 to -521
http://tennessee.gov/consumer/documents/LandlordTenant
Brochure.pdf

Texas
Texas Property Code Ann. §§ 91.001 to 92.354
http://tlo2.tlc.state.tx.us/statutes/pr.toc.htm

Attorney General: Tenant Rights
http://www.oag.state.tx.us/AG_Publications/pdfs/tenant_rights.pdf

Utah
Utah Code Ann. §§ 57-17-1 to -5; §§ 57-22-1 to -6
http://www.le.state.ut.us/~code/TITLE57/TITLE57.htm

Utah State Courts
http://www.utcourts.gov/howto/landlord/

Vermont
Vermont Statutes Ann. Title 9, Chapter 137 §§ 4451 to 4468 (Residential
Rental Agreements)

http://www.leg.state.vt.us/statutes/sections.cfm?Title=09&
   Chapter=137

"Police Response in Illegal Evictions" by Champlain Valley Office of
Economic Opportunity
   http://www.cvoeo.org/htm/Housing/tenants/police.html

Virginia
Virginia Residential Landlord and Tenant Act
   http://www.dhcd.virginia.gov/HomelessnesstoHomeownership/
      PDFs/Landlord_Tenant_Handbook.pdf

Virginia Code Ann. §§ 55-218.1 to -248.40
   http://leg1.state.va.us/cgi-bin/legp504.exe?000+cod+TOC550000000
      13000020000000

Washington
Attorney General
   http://atg.wa.gov/ResidentialLT/default.aspx

Washington Rev. Code Ann. §§ 59.04.010 to .900; §§ 59.18.010 to .911
   http://apps.leg.wa.gov/RCW/default.aspx?cite=59.18

West Virginia
"Decent Housing Is a Right"
   http://www.wvago.gov/pdf/Tenants_rights.pdf

City of Charleston: Landlord/Tenant Responsibilities
   http://www.cityofcharleston.org/documents/landlordtenant.pdf

West Virginia Code §§ 37-6-1 to -30
   http://www.charlestonhousing.com/WV%20Code%20Landlord-
      Tenant%20Laws.pdf

Wisconsin
Wisconsin Statutes Ann. §§ 704.01-.50
   http://www.legis.state.wi.us/statutes/Stat0704.pdf

Wisconsin Administrative Code 134.01 to .10
   http://www.legis.state.wi.us/rsb/code/atcp/atcp134.pdf

Wisconsin State Law Library
http://wsll.state.wi.us/topic/landlord.html

Wyoming

Wyoming Statutes Title 1, Article 21 §§ 1201 to 1211
http://legisweb.state.wy.us/statutes/dlstatutes.htm

University of Wyoming: Students' Attorney on Eviction
http://uwacadweb.uwyo.edu/studentatty/viewcat.asp?id=42

Websites That Contain Information of Interest

Better Business Bureau
http://www.bbb.com

Credit Bureaus
EQUIFAX – PO Box 740256, Atlanta, GA 30374-0256
   1-800-685-1111
   http://www.equifax.com

EXPERIAN – PO Box 2104, Allen, TX 75013-2104
   1-888-397-3742
   http://www.experian.com

TRANS UNION – PO Box 1000, Chester, PA 19022
   1-800-888-4213
   http://www.tuc.com

Companion Animals/Pet Information
   http://www.peoplewithpets.com
   http://www.apartmentdog.com
   http://www.petrent.net
   http://www.rentersonly.net

http://www.treehouseanimals.org
http://www.drsfostersmith.com

Government Information and Federal Laws

http://www.access-board.gov/about/laws/ABA.htm
http://www.ada.gov/pubs/ada.htm
http://www.dol.gov/oasam/regs/statutes/age_act.htm
http://www.epa.gov
http://www.epa.gov/lead/nlic.htm
http://www.firstgov.gov
http://www.hud.gov/local/index.cfm
http://www.hud.gov/offices/fheo/FHLaws/yourrights.cfm
http://www.hud.gov/offices/fheo/FHLaws/109.cfm
http://www.hud.gov/renting
http://www.makinghomeaffordable.gov
http://www.osha.gov
http://www.usdoj.gov/crt/cor/coord/titleixstat.htm
http://www.usdoj.gov/crt/grants_statutes/titlevi.txt
http://www.usdoj.gov/crt/housing/title8.htm

Hazards: Lead Paint, Mold, Asbestos

http://www.epa.gov
http://www.epa.gov/lead/nlic.htm
http://www.osha.gov

Office of Healthy Homes and Lead Hazard Control - U.S. Department of Housing and Urban Development (HUD)
http://www.hud.gov/offices/lead/

Indoor Air Quality and State Radon Office Locator - U.S. Environmental Protection Agency (EPA)
http://www.epa.gov/iaq/contacts.html

Mold Dangers and Resources-U.S. Environmental Protection Agency (EPA)
http://www.epa.gov/mold/moldresources.html

Landlord Organizations

http://www.landlordassociation.org
http://www.rentalagreements.net

http://www.thelpa.com
http://www.landlord.com

Legal Assistance

http://www.sphinxlegal.com
http://www.abanet.org
http://www.findgreatlawyers.com
http://www.findlaw.com
http://www.lawguru.com
http://www.law.com
http://www.rentlaw.com

Property Managers

The National Association of Residential Property Managers (NARPM)
http://www.narpm.org

Rentometer

Compare rents in a particular area
http://www.rentometer.com

Vacation Rentals

http://www.homeaway.com
http://www.zonder.com

Forms

This section contains the basic generic forms that are presented for the landlord's use. You may copy them, alter them, or use them to create forms that are applicable to your situation, location, and local laws. You may want to begin by scanning or typing the form into your word processor software. Letters to your tenants should be printed on letterhead that has the landlord's contact information pre-printed on the paper.

Remember, every state has its own requirements on what should be included in important forms such as leases, agreement, and notices. Some counties and cities also have certain legal requirements. No generic form will ever be able to comply with the laws for fifty states and countless cities/counties that have enacted laws governing the landlord-tenant situation.

INDEX OF FORMS

- PROSPECTIVE TENANT SYSTEM

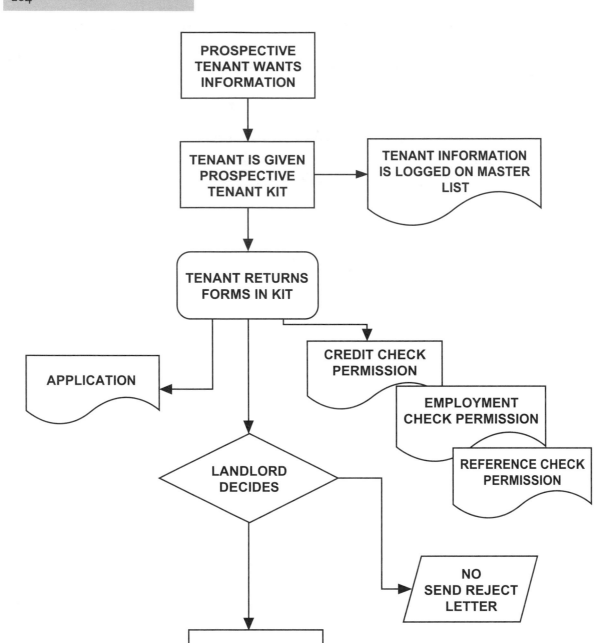

PROSPECTIVE TENANT MASTER LIST

DATE	TENANT NAME	CONTACT INFO	APPLIC. DATE	ACCEPT/ REJECT	DATE
/ /			/ /		/ /
/ /			/ /		/ /
/ /			/ /		/ /
/ /			/ /		/ /
/ /			/ /		/ /
/ /			/ /		/ /
/ /			/ /		/ /
/ /			/ /		/ /
/ /			/ /		/ /
/ /			/ /		/ /
/ /			/ /		/ /
/ /			/ /		/ /
/ /			/ /		/ /
/ /			/ /		/ /
/ /			/ /		/ /
/ /			/ /		/ /
/ /			/ /		/ /
/ /			/ /		/ /

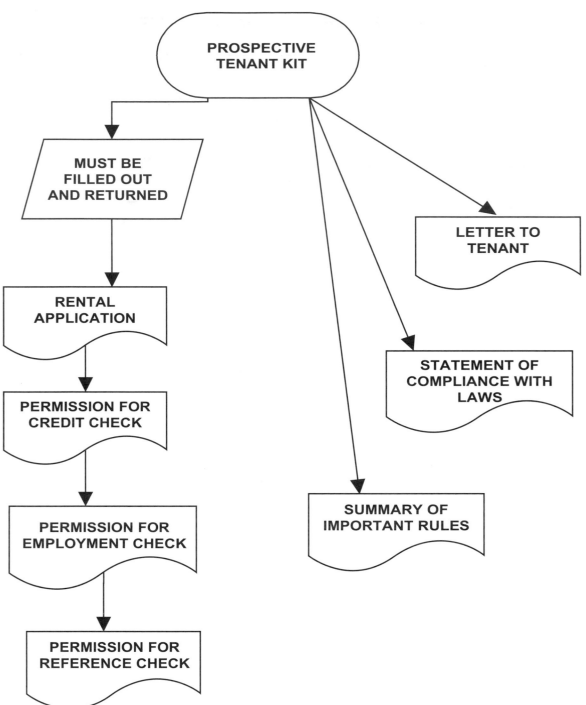

LETTER TO PROSPECTIVE TENANT

Dear Prospective Tenant:

Thank you for considering rental of our property at:

_____

_____.

We will be evaluating you at the same time that we invite you to evaluate us. For our evaluation we have requested that you provide us with basic information in a rental application, with references, and with permission to run a credit check and an employment check on you and any others who will be signing our lease.

To help you evaluate us we are providing you with information on our non-discrimination practices and a list of some of the more important rules that are enforced.

If we come to a mutual agreement regarding your tenancy, you may be provided with additional forms to fill out regarding companion animals, you will be provided with a complete list of our rules in detail, and you will be asked to sign a rental agreement or lease.

We will process your rental application as soon as possible. We estimate that we will contact you on _____ with our decision. Until then, we will provide you with any information on our rental that you request. Please contact _____ at _____ - _____ with any questions.

Sincerely,

Landlord

RENTAL APPLICATION

PROSPECTIVE TENANT APPLICATION		
Tenant Information		
Name:		
Date of Birth:	SSN:	Phone:
Current address:		
City:	State	ZIP Code:
Own Rent (Please circle)	Monthly Payment or rent:	How long?
Previous Address:		
City:	State:	ZIP Code:
Owned Rented (Please circle)	Monthly Payment or rent:	How long?
Employment Information		
Current Employer:		
Employer Address:		How long?
Phone	E-mail:	Fax:
City:	State:	ZIP Code:
Position:	Hourly Salary (Please circle)	Annual Income:
No. of people applying as tenant(s):	No. of children (under 18):	
Cotenant Information		
Name:		
Date of Birth:	SSN:	Phone:
Current address:		
City:	State:	ZIP Code:
Own Rent (Please circle)	Monthly Payment or rent:	How long?
Previous Address:		
City:	State:	ZIP Code:
Owned Rented (Please circle)	Monthly Payment or rent:	How long?
Co-applicant Employment Information		
Current Employer:		
Employer Address:		How long?
Phone	E-mail:	Fax:
City:	State:	ZIP Code:
Position:	Hourly Salary (Please circle)	Annual Income:
References		
Name:	Address:	Phone:
I authorize the verification of the information provided on this form, including investigation as to my credit, employment, and contact of my references.		
Signature of prospective tenant:		Date:
Signature of cotenant:		Date:

NON-DISCRIMINATION STATEMENT

TO WHOM IT MAY CONCERN:

We do not discriminate in the rental of this property. We do not discriminate against tenants or potential tenants due to their race, color, national origin, religion, sex, family status or disability. This rental proudly follows all state and federal fair housing laws including the Fair Housing Act, Title VI of the Civil Rights Act, Americans with Disabilities Act, and the Age Discrimination Act.

_____

(signed by owner/landlord)

POTENTIAL TENANT CONSENT

AUTHORIZATION FOR REFERENCE CHECK
NOTE: ALL cotenants must fill out individual forms)

NAME: _____

ADDRESS: _____

_____

REFERENCES:

Last Name	First Name	Middle Initial

Street

City	State	Zip

Phone	Fax

E-mail

Last Name	First Name	Middle Initial

Street

City	State	Zip

Phone	Fax

E-mail

By signing below I authorize the landlord or his/her agent to contact the above references, to contact my employer as listed on the Application, and to perform a complete credit check on myself.

Signature	Date

SUMMARY OF IMPORTANT RULES
(Sample)

Dear Potential Tenant:

As you complete your application to occupy our rental property, we want you to be aware of some of our rules. If you do rent from us, a complete set of rules will be provided for you when you sign the rental lease.

- Rent is due on the first of every month. Rent payments are considered late if the landlord does not receive them by the fifth of every month. A $5 late charge will be assessed for the first late payment, thereafter the late charge will be increased to $20. Frequent late rent payments can result in the termination of the lease upon proper legal notice to the tenant, and/or non-renewal of future leases.
- Tenants are responsible for all damage that they do to the rental unit, even if the damage is not intentional. Tenants are urged to repair damage as it occurred, or contact the landlord to have the damage repaired at the cost of the tenant. The cost of repairing damages at the end of the lease will be deducted from the tenant's security deposit.
- Tenants are assigned one numbered parking place close to the entry of their unit. Tenants must register their vehicle with the landlord and display the Property sticker on the front windshield. Visitors are required to park in the lot indicated as 'visitors parking'.
- Tenants must not leave items in the hallways or in the common areas without permission of the landlord.
- This rental property strictly follows the local laws regarding noise. This means that if your neighbors can hear your party, TV, music, etc. after 10 p.m. on weekdays and 11 p.m. on weekends; and before 7 a.m. on weekdays and 8 a.m. on weekends, you are in violation of the law. All tenant complaints regarding other tenant's violations of the rules will be investigated.
- Tenants who routinely violate the rules of this property are subject to having their lease terminated and/or non-renewal of future leases.

NOTICE OF DENIAL TO PROSPECTIVE TENANT

Date: _____

Dear _____,

Thank you for applying to rent the property at:

_____

_____.

Unfortunately at this time we are unable to offer you a lease for this property. We wish you the very best in obtaining a rental that will be suitable for your needs.

Sincerely,

Landlord or property manager

NOTICE OF CONDITIONAL ACCEPTANCE

Date: _____

Dear _____,

It is our pleasure to inform you that you have been approved to rent the property at:

_____

_____

The next step is for you to come in the office and sign the Rental Agreement. At that time we will need your first month's rent payment, plus the security deposit. If you have arranged for a Companion Animal addition to your lease, we will need the security deposit for that agreement at that time also. Once these items are taken care of, you can schedule a move-in.

When you determine your move in date, we will reserve the freight elevator for your use from 6 a.m. until 11 p.m. on that day. As a courtesy to our other tenants, we do not allow move-ins prior to 6 a.m. or after 11 p.m. If you are utilizing professional movers we can reserve a dock for the moving truck in our delivery area.

Please call our office to set up a time when we can sign the Rental Agreement and provide you with the other paperwork as a tenant. If we do not hear from you within ten days from the above date, we will assume that you no need this rental and will select another tenant.

Sincerely,

Landlord

NEW TENANT PROCEDURE

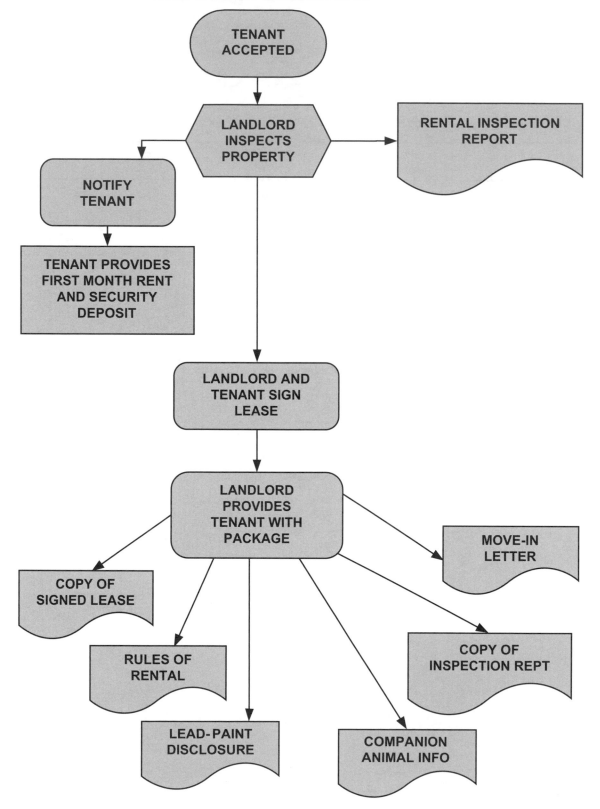

TENANT
ACCEPTED

LANDLORD
INSPECTS
PROPERTY

RENTAL INSPECTION
REPORT

NOTIFY
TENANT

TENANT PROVIDES
FIRST MONTH RENT
AND SECURITY
DEPOSIT

LANDLORD AND
TENANT SIGN
LEASE

LANDLORD
PROVIDES
TENANT WITH
PACKAGE

MOVE-IN
LETTER

COPY OF
SIGNED LEASE

RULES OF
RENTAL

COPY OF
INSPECTION REPT

LEAD-PAINT
DISCLOSURE

COMPANION
ANIMAL INFO

RENTAL PROPERTY INSPECTION REPORT

This form is used by the landlord prior to the tenant moving in as a way to assess the condition of the details of the rental unit. A copy is then provided to the tenant prior to move in. If the tenant observes something that is in need of repair, the tenant should note that on the form and return the form to the landlord. The last column on this form is for the landlord to calculate damage, if any, when this tenant moves out.

CONDITION =   ✓   OK
              R   needs repair
              M   missing, needs replacement
              N/A not intended to be in rental property

ITEM DESCRIPTION	MOVE-IN CONDITION	MOVE-OUT CONDITION	$$$
ENTRYWAY-OUTSIDE			
Door			
Locks			
Security peephole			
Lighting			
ENTRYWAY-INSIDE			
Door			
Securlty chain or deadbolt			
Door secure in frame			
KITCHEN			
Flooring/carpet/tile			
Walls			
Ceiling/ceiling light			
Cabinets/shelves			
Counters			
Stove/oven			
Range hood			
Kitchen fire extinguisher			
Refrigerator			
Sink			
Water supply			

Continued

Gas supply			
Electricity			
Dishwasher			
Windows			
Doorway			
Furniture			
DINING AREA/DINING ROOM			
Flooring/carpet/tile			
Walls			
Ceiling/ceiling light			
Furniture			
Electrical access			
Windows			
LIVING/FAMILY ROOM			
Flooring/carpet/tile			
Walls			
Ceiling/ceiling light			
Furniture			
Electrical access			
Windows			
BATHROOM #1			
Flooring/carpet/tile			
Walls			
Ceiling/ceiling light			
Window			
Electrical access			
Sink		.	
Toilet			
Bathtub/shower			

Continued

Water access			
Drainage			
BATHROOM #2			
Flooring/carpet/tile			
Walls			
Ceiling/ceiling light			
Window			
Electrical access			
Sink			
Toilet			
Bathtub/shower			
Water access			
Drainage			
BEDROOM #1			
Flooring/carpet/tile			
Walls			
Ceiling/ceiling light			
Window			
Electrical access			
Furniture			
Closets/shelves/clothes rod			
Smoke Detector			
BEDROOM #2			
Flooring/carpet/tile			
Walls			
Ceiling/ceiling light			
Window			
Electrical access			
Furniture			

Continued

Closets/shelves/clothes rod			
Smoke detector			
BEDROOM #3			
Flooring/carpet/tile			
Walls			
Ceiling/ceiling light			
Window			
Electrical access			
Furniture			
Closets/shelves/clothes rod			
Smoke detector			
MISCELLANEOUS			
Heating unit			
Air conditioner			
Carbon monoxide detector			
Hot water heater			
Access to fuse/circuit breakers			
Driveway/parking spot			
Garbage container			

The landlord certifies that he/she has inspected each item listed on this form and has given it an accurate rating. If tenant disagrees, please make note of on that on this form and contact the landlord. If the landlord does not receive tenant's complaint within 48 hours of tenant's moving in, landlord will assume that the tenant accepts landlord's assessment of these items.

Date Reviewed: _____

Landlord: _____

RESIDENTIAL RENTAL LEASE

This agreement is made this _____ day of _____, 20 _____.

In consideration of mutual covenants and agreements as contained herein Tenant(s): _____

_____

hereby leases from Landlord:

_____

the residential property at:

_____

_____

Landlord and Tenant mutually covenant, promise and agree as follows:

1. TERM OF LEASE The terms of the Agreement is for _____ months, the Agreement begins on _____ and terminates at midnight on the last day of the term of this Agreement on _____. (Options: can change this for a month-to-month or a limited time lease)

2. RENT Tenant shall pay Landlord for the use and occupancy of the leased residential premises the sum of $ _____ per _____. The rent should be paid to the Landlord at the above address.

3. INITIAL PAYMENT BY TENANT. Tenant shall pay the amount of the first rental payment of $ _____ plus a Security Deposit of $ _____ to the Landlord to initiate this lease.

4. SECURITY DEPOSIT. Tenant has deposited with Landlord the sum of $ _____ plus an additional amount of $ _____ for (animal damage deposit/garage deposit/storage deposit). These deposits shall be held by Landlord in accordance with the laws of the state of _____ regarding security deposits for rentals. These deposits are to be used to repair damages (not common wear and tear) that the Tenant inflicted upon the rental property. Within thirty (30) days after Tenant has surrendered the property to Landlord, the Landlord will make an inspection of the premises and determine if any of these deposit monies will be needed to repair damage. Landlord will then return the unused portion of the deposits to the Tenant, with an itemized list of repairs made. The security deposit is NOT to be used for the last month's rent.

5. PROPERTY USE. Tenant agrees to use the premises for residential purposes only. Tenant further agrees to use the leased premises in a manner that will not violate any federal, state, or local laws or regulations.

6. TENANT'S OCCUPANCY. Tenant agrees that only those who are listed on this document, identified as Tenant(s) shall occupy the leased premises during the term of this agreement.

- -

SUGGESTED CLAUSES

a. **MAINTENANCE CLAUSE** Tenant has examined the property and acknowledges it to be in good repair. OPTIONAL: In consideration of a reduced rental rate, Tenant agrees to keep the premises in repair and to do all minor maintenance promptly, paying for both materials and labor. OR Tenant agrees to promptly report any broken items or those in need of repair directly to the Landlord who will arrange for maintenance on the rental property.

b. **LIABILITY** Tenant agrees that Landlord has advised Tenant to obtain standard rental insurance. Tenant agrees to indemnify and hold Landlord harmless from and against all claims arising from any act, omission, or negligence of Tenant or Tenant's licensees or invitees that may occur inor about the leased premises during the term of this

Agreement., and from and against all costs, expenses, liabilities incurred in or in connection with any such claim or proceeding brought thereon including attorneys fees incurred in connection therewith.

c. **INSURANCE** Tenant acknowledges that Landlord has advised Tenant to obtain standard rental insurance. Landlord has advised Tenant that Tenant will be responsible to the maximum extent for any loss that would have been covered by such an insurance policy.

d. **ASSIGNMENT and SUBLEASE** Tenant shall not transfer, assign, sub-lease or add another Tenant to this agreement without the expressed permission of the Landlord.

e. **ABANDONMENT** Landlord will consider the rental property abandoned when Tenant is thirty days late on rent AND Landlord is unable to contact Tenant at the rental property or at the place of employment listed on the rental application. Landlord then has the option to hold Tenant in default and to initiate any appropriate legal action.

f. **LATE PAYMENTS** If the monthly rental payment is not received by the Landlord by midnight on the first day of each month a late charge in the amount of $ _____ will be assessed and immediately due and owing. An additional $ _____ will be assessed and immediately due and owing if the Landlord serves the Tenant with a Three-Day Notice to Vacate.

g. **CHANGING LOCKS ON RENTAL PROPERTY** Tenant shall not change the locks on the rental property without the expressed permission of the Landlord. If the Tenant is involved in a domestic abuse dispute and can comply with the requirements of the state law which provides a party involved in domestic abuse with certain benefits, the Landlord will provide a new lock at no charge to the Tenant. Tenant(s) who do not qualify under the domestic abuse laws, can request that the Landlord change the locks. In those cases the Tenant will only be charged with the cost of materials, not the cost of labor to change the locks. Should the Tenant, without permission of the Landlord, change the locks on the rental property, the Tenant will be charge with both materials and labor to replace the locks. If this is not identified until after the Tenant has vacated the premises, this cost will be subtracted from any security deposit.

h. **PARKING** Tenant will be assigned parking spots #_____, #_____. Additional vehicles and visitors vehicles must be parked in the visitor's lot. Tenant's vehicles must display the parking pass on the front windshield. Tenants can purchase covered garage spot for $ _____ per month. Tenants can purchase a storage spot for RVs, boats, etc. for $ _____ per month. The covered garage and storage spots are sold on a first-come, first-served basis.

i. **STORAGE** Tenant receives one _____ foot by _____ foot locked cage area for storage. The storage cages are located _____. What can be placed in these storage cages is subject to federal, state and local laws; please see posted signs for items that cannot be placed in this storage area. Tenant assumes the full liability of all damage caused by items placed in the storage cage.

j. **UTILITIES** Landlord is responsible for the payment of gas, water, and electricity. OR Landlord is responsible for the payment of _____, Tenant is responsible for payment of _____. OTHER OPTIONS: Landlord shall arrange to have the above services put in the name of the Tenant beginning on the move-in date. Tenant is responsible for all billing of that service from move-in date to the end of the tenancy.

k. **ALTERATIONS** Tenant shall not make any permanent alterations on the rental premises without the express permission of the Landlord. This includes painting, installation of stabilizing bars in the bathtub, and all other improvements. For some improvements, the Landlord will assume a portion of the cost. Improvements or changes made to the premises without the express permission of the Landlord may be removed at the end of the tenancy and that cost deducted from the Tenant's security deposit.

l. **ABANDONED PROPERTY** Any personal property that the Tenant leaves on the rental premises at the end of the tenancy, upon abandonment of the rental, or upon eviction, will be stored by the Landlord for a period of no longer than ten (10) days. If the Tenant does not retrieve the property at the end of that time the Landlord will take possession of the property and dispose of the property as the Landlord sees fit.

m. **RETURN OF SECURITY DEPOSIT** The security deposit shall be held by Landlord in accordance with the laws of the state of _____ regarding security deposits for rentals. At the end of the rental term, the deposit will be used to cover the repair of any damages (not common wear and tear) that the Tenant inflicted upon the rental property. The Landlord calculates this damage amount using the Premises Inventory form and other evidence. The cost of repair is determined by cost of materials, cost of labor, and/or estimates to repair. Within thirty (30) days after Tenant has surrendered the property to Landlord, the Landlord will make an inspection of the premises and determine if any of these deposit monies will be needed to repair damage. Landlord will then return the unused portion of the deposits to the Tenant, with an itemized list of repairs made. The security deposit is **NOT** to be used for the last month's rent.

n. **ENTRY and INSPECTIONS** Tenant agrees that the Landlord and his agents shall have the right to enter leased premises during normal business hours at any time during an emergency or after Tenant has abandoned the rental property. For all other entries Tenant will receive a 24 hour notice prior to entry. In cases of the Tenant's request for maintenance or repair, Tenant can wave the 24 hour wait before entry.

o. **OTHER AREAS** Tenant specifically leases the rental premises as identified in this document. In addition Landlord grants Tenant the use of all common areas such as: always, stairs, entryway, mail room, laundry room, passenger elevator, and outside grounds. Use of the freight elevator is requested through the Landlord or his/her agents.

p. **RETURN OF PREMISES** Tenant agrees to return the leased premises to the Landlord at the end of the tenancy, as indicated in this document. Thirty days prior to the end of the tenancy Landlord and Tenant may negotiate a renewal lease. The terms of the renewal lease are determined at the time of that negotiation. At thirty days prior to the end of the tenancy the Tenant must notify the Landlord if he/she intends to move-out at the end of the lease. Tenants who do not leave at the end of this lease and who are not offered a renewal lease will automatically be subject to a month-to-month tenancy with an increase of 25% in the amount of monthly rent payment.

q. **SMOKING** Tenant shall not smoke or permit any guests or invitees to smoke cigarettes, pipes, cigars or other smoking material inside the leased premises.

r. **SALE OF PREMISES** In the event of the sale, voluntary or involuntary, transfer, or assignment of the Landlord's interest in the leased premises during the term of this Agreement; this Agreement shall operate to release the current Landlord from any future liability under the Agreement. This Agreement is, so far as allowed under the law, binding upon all successors of the Landlord.

s. **DEFAULTS** If the Tenant has defaulted on this agreement by not paying rent or by violation of the Rules, the Landlord reserves the option to evict the Tenant from the premises using the appropriate legal procedures.

t. **RULES OF THE RENTAL PREMISES** This Agreement incorporates the document entitled RULES as part of this contract.

u. **RULES ON PETS** This Agreement incorporates the document entitled RULES ON COMPANION ANIMALS or RULES ON PETS as part of this contract.

v. **GOVERNING LAWS** This Agreement shall be governed by, construed, and enforced in accordance with the laws and legal decision of the State of _____.

w. **FAIR HOUSING** Both Landlord and Tenant understand the State and Federal Housing Laws prohibit discrimination in the leasing of housing on the basis of race, religion, color, sex, familial status, sexual preference, disability, or national origin.

IN WITNESS THEREOF, the parties have read, understand, and do hereby execute this Agreement on the date written above.

LANDLORD: TENANT(S)

_____   _____

                                                  _____

                                                  _____

                                                  _____

CREDIT COSIGNER FOR RENTAL

CREDIT COSIGNER FOR RENTAL

_____   _____   _____
Last Name   First Name   Middle Initial

_____
Street

_____   _____   _____
City   State   Zip

_____   _____
Phone   Fax

_____
E-mail

Social Security#

_____

— —

I hereby agree to co-sign for _____
in his/her application to rent the premises that are located at:

_____

_____

I understand that by co-signing, I agree to pay all rental fees, security deposits, and damages that are due an owing from the above referenced tenancy.

_____   ____/____/____

Signature   Month / Day / Year

DISCLOSURE OF LEAD-BASED PAINT

Disclosure of Information on Lead-Based Paint and/or Lead-Based Paint Hazards

Housing built before 1978 may contain lead-based paint. Lead from paint, paint chips, and dust can pose health hazards if not managed properly. Lead exposure is especially harmful to young children and pregnant women. Before renting pre-1978 housing, lessors must disclose the presence of known lead-based paint and/or lead-based paint hazards in the dwelling. Lessees must also receive a federally approved pamphlet on lead poisoning prevention.

Lessor's (LANDLORD) Disclosure   (check (i) or (ii) below)

(a) Presence of lead-based paint and/or lead-based paint hazards (check (i) or (ii) below):

   (i) _____ Known lead-based paint and/or lead-based paint hazards are present in the housing (explain).

   (ii) _____ Lessor has no knowledge of lead-based paint and/or lead-based paint hazards in the housing.

(b) Records and reports available to the lessor:

   (i) _____ Lessor has provided the lessee with all available records and reports pertaining to lead-based paint and/or lead-based paint hazards in the housing (list documents below).

   (ii) _____ Lessor has no reports or records pertaining to lead-based paint and/or lead-based paint hazards in the housing.

Lessee's (TENANT) Acknowledgment (initial)

(c) _____ Lessee has received copies of all information listed above.

(d) _____ Lessee has received the pamphlet Protect Your Family from Lead in Your Home.

Agent's Acknowledgment (initial)

(e) _____ Agent has informed the lessor of the lessor's obligations under 42 U.S.C. 4852d and is aware of his/her responsibility to ensure compliance.

Certification of Accuracy

The following parties have reviewed the information above and certify, to the best of their knowledge, that the information they have provided is true and accurate.

_____   _____
                LANDLORD   **DATE**

_____   _____
                 TENANT   **DATE**

MOVE-IN LETTER

Date: _____

Dear _____,

Congratulations on becoming one of our valued tenants. We hope that this will be the beginning of a terrific relationship.

Enclosed in this packet is:

- A copy of the signed rental agreement
- The rules of the rental property
- A copy of the inspection report for your rental
- And other documents that may be applicable to your rental—lead paint disclosure, companion animal documents, storage information, garage information

We ask that you read all the enclosed documents and if you have any questions, please contact us. We look forward to making you feel right at home here.

Sincerely,

Landlord

COMPANION ANIMAL REFERENCE / APPLICATION

TENANT INFORMATION:

Name : _____

Address: _____

_____

PET(S) INFORMATION:

1. Name   Type   Age

   _____   _____   _____

   _____   _____   _____

   _____   _____   _____

2. Veterinarian: _____

3. List references who know your pet (former landlord, veterinarian)

_____

_____

_____

_____

_____   _____

TENANT   **DATE**

COMPANION ANIMAL AGREEMENT

THIS AGREEMENT was freely entered into on _____ between
_____ (Landlord) and _____ (Tenant(s)).
It is an addition to and part of the Residential Rental Lease that exists between these parties.

In consideration of $ _____ as a non-refundable cleaning payment and of payment of $ _____ as an addition
security deposit for damages caused by the listed companion animal(s), tenant is allowed to keep companion animals
on the rental premises under the following conditions:

1. Tenant agrees to keep all areas where any pets are housed clean and free from parasites, including fleas.

2. Tenant agrees to provide one litter box per cat, and a piddle-pan for dogs not housebroken.

3. Tenant agrees that all pets will receive proper veterinary care, including all legally required inoculation and will wear
an identification tag and/or microchip identification.

4. No pet is to be left alone for a period longer than that which is appropriate according to the needs of the individual
pet. Although this period may vary depending upon the particular pet, it is agreed that, in general, dogs should not be
left alone for more than ten hours, and other pets for longer than twenty-four hours on a regular basis.

5. Tenant agrees to provide landlord with information as to an emergency contact and name of the veterinarian who
is familiar with the pet, should there be an emergency where immediate pet assistance is needed.

6. Tenant agrees to keep the pet on a leash and to accompany the pet for daily walks. Tenant agrees to clean up
after his/her pet's defecation and other waste. Tenant agrees to be financially responsible for any property destroyed
by the pet.

7. Tenant agrees to work with the landlord in resolving any complaints for other residents.

_____   _____
LANDLORD   **DATE**

_____   _____
TENANT   **DATE**

PROPERTY MANAGER NOTIFICATION

Date: _____

TO ALL TENANTS;

Starting today, _____ is joining our rental team as my agent in the position of Property Manager for these premises.

_____ will handle all requests for repairs and maintenance; he/she is also authorized to collect monthly rental payments. Please direct all questions to _____ at _____ - _____.

OR

Starting today, this rental property will be managed by the Property Management Company of _____.

They will act as my agent and will handle all requests for repairs and maintenance, in addition to collecting monthly rental payments. Please direct all questions to _____ at _____ - _____.

Sincerely,

Landlord

AMENDMENT TO LEASE OR RENTAL AGREEMENT

This agreement is made this _____ day of _____, 20 _____.

In consideration of mutual covenants and agreements as contained herein Tenant(s): _____

_____

hereby leases from Landlord:

_____

the residential property at:

_____

_____

Landlord and Tenant mutually covenant, promise and agree as follows:

1. AMENDMENT TO RENTAL LEASE This document is to act as an amendment to the Residential Rental Agreement that these parties entered into on _____.

2. AMENDMENT

_____

_____

_____

_____

_____

_____

WITH BOTH PARTIES IN AGREEMENT, on the above date they legally bind themselves by signature.

_____   _____
LANDLORD   **DATE**

_____   _____
TENANT   **DATE**

AGREEMENT FOR ALTERATIONS TO RENTAL AGREEMENT REGARDING ASSIGNMENT

This agreement is made this ⎯⎯⎯⎯ day of ⎯⎯⎯⎯⎯⎯⎯⎯ , 20 ⎯⎯⎯ .

In consideration of mutual covenants and agreements as contained herein Tenant(s): ⎯⎯⎯⎯⎯⎯⎯⎯

⎯⎯⎯⎯⎯⎯⎯⎯⎯⎯⎯⎯⎯⎯⎯⎯⎯⎯⎯⎯⎯⎯⎯⎯⎯⎯⎯⎯⎯⎯⎯

hereby leases from Landlord:

⎯⎯⎯⎯⎯⎯⎯⎯⎯⎯⎯⎯⎯⎯⎯⎯⎯⎯⎯⎯⎯⎯⎯⎯⎯⎯⎯⎯⎯⎯⎯

the residential property at:

⎯⎯⎯⎯⎯⎯⎯⎯⎯⎯⎯⎯⎯⎯⎯⎯⎯⎯⎯⎯⎯⎯⎯⎯⎯⎯⎯⎯⎯⎯⎯

⎯⎯⎯⎯⎯⎯⎯⎯⎯⎯⎯⎯⎯⎯⎯⎯⎯⎯⎯⎯⎯⎯⎯⎯⎯⎯⎯⎯⎯⎯⎯

Landlord and Tenant mutually covenant, promise and agree as follows:

1. ALTERATION TO RENTAL LEASE This document is to act as an addendum to the Residential Rental Agreement that these parties entered into on ⎯⎯⎯⎯⎯⎯⎯⎯ .

2. ASSIGNMENT Tenant has requested the following person(s) be assigned all the responsibilities and duties that are contained in the above referenced Residential Rental Agreement.

⎯⎯⎯⎯⎯⎯⎯⎯⎯⎯⎯⎯⎯⎯⎯⎯⎯⎯⎯⎯⎯⎯⎯

⎯⎯⎯⎯⎯⎯⎯⎯⎯⎯⎯⎯⎯⎯⎯⎯⎯⎯⎯⎯⎯⎯⎯

⎯⎯⎯⎯⎯⎯⎯⎯⎯⎯⎯⎯⎯⎯⎯⎯⎯⎯⎯⎯⎯⎯⎯

⎯⎯⎯⎯⎯⎯⎯⎯⎯⎯⎯⎯⎯⎯⎯⎯⎯⎯⎯⎯⎯⎯⎯

3. LIABILITY Tenant agrees that if the above assignee does not follow the requirements as listed in the Rental Agreement, the Landlord can hold the tenant financially responsible for all liability.

WITH BOTH PARTIES IN AGREEMENT, on the above date they legally bind themselves by signature.

⎯⎯⎯⎯⎯⎯⎯⎯⎯⎯⎯⎯⎯⎯⎯⎯⎯   ⎯⎯⎯⎯⎯⎯⎯
LANDLORD   **DATE**

⎯⎯⎯⎯⎯⎯⎯⎯⎯⎯⎯⎯⎯⎯⎯⎯⎯   ⎯⎯⎯⎯⎯⎯⎯
TENANT   **DATE**

RESIDENT'S MAINTENANCE AND REPAIR REQUEST

Date: _____

From: _____

Unit #: _____ Daytime Phone: _____ - _____

I need the following repair/maintenance in the above rental unit:

_____

_____

_____

_____

_____

_____

Need repair/maintenance done by: _____.

_____
TENANT

Resolution:

_____

_____

_____

_____

_____

_____

AGREEMENT REGARDING TENANT ALTERATIONS

This agreement is made this _____ day of _____, 20 _____.

In consideration of mutual covenants and agreements as contained herein Tenant(s): _____

_____

hereby leases from Landlord:

_____

the residential property at:

_____

_____

Landlord and Tenant mutually covenant, promise and agree as follows:

1. ADDENDUM TO RENTAL LEASE This document is to act as an addendum to the Residential Rental Agreement that these parties entered into on _____.

2. REQUEST FOR ALTERATION Tenant has requested the following alteration to the rental premises:

_____

_____

_____

_____

_____

_____

{Attach all drawings, blueprints, estimates to this document.}

3. AGREEMENT Landlord has agreed to the alteration under the following terms. OPTIONAL CLAUSES:

- Tenant pays for materials and labor
- Landlord pays for materials and labor
- Landlord pays _____ % of total for materials and labor.
- Landlord arranges to have alteration done by contractor or property handy-person
- Tenant removes alteration at the end of his/her tenancy
- Cost of removal is Tenant's responsibility and may become a deduction from the security deposit
- Alteration remains with the premises
- For alterations that become a permanent part of the premises, Landlord pays Tenant $ _____ for the improvement.

WITH BOTH PARTIES IN AGREEMENT, on the above date they legally bind themselves by signature.

_____   _____
LANDLORD   **DATE**

_____   _____
TENANT   **DATE**

NOTICE OF INTENT TO ENTER PREMISES

Date: _____

To: _____

On _____ at _____ am/pm, it will be necessary to enter the rental premises for:

☐ Tenant's request for repair/maintenance

☐ Necessary repair/maintenance on the premises

☐ Landlord's inspection of premises

☐ City/state required inspection

☐ Other: _____

In the event that this is not convenient, please call to arrange another time.

_____   _____ - _____
LANDLORD   PHONE

AGREEMENT TO TERMINATE LEASE

This agreement is made this _____ day of _____ , 20 _____ .

In consideration of mutual covenants and agreements as contained herein Tenant(s): _____

_____

hereby leases from Landlord:

_____

the residential property at:

_____

_____

Landlord and Tenant mutually covenant, promise and agree as follows:

1. AMEND RENTAL LEASE This document is to act as an amendment to the Residential Rental Agreement that these parties entered into on _____ .

2. NEW TERMINATION DATE Tenant and Landlord agree that the new termination date on the Rental Agreement is _____ . List other changes to Agreement here:

_____

_____

_____

_____

WITH BOTH PARTIES IN AGREEMENT, on the above date they legally bind themselves by signature.

_____   _____

LANDLORD   **DATE**

_____   _____

TENANT   **DATE**

WARNING LETTER FOR LEASE
OR RENTAL AGREEMENT VIOLATION

Date: _____

Dear _____,

It has come to our attention that you are in violation of the Rules of the rental property as contained in your lease. These violations are:

_____

_____

_____

_____

_____

_____

As you are undoubtedly aware, a violation of the rules listed in the lease can result in your eviction, or other penalties. In order to continue the pleasant atmosphere of this rental community we all must abide by the rules. If you continue to violate the rules we will be forced to take legal action to have you removed from the rental premises in accordance with the lease that you signed.

Sincerely,

Landlord

LETTER REGARDING PAST-DUE RENT

Date: _____

Dear _____,

It has come to our attention that you are in violation of the rules of the rental property, as contained in your lease, due to your non-payment of rent. This is a very serious offense and one that will not be tolerated. In accordance with the terms of payment as stated in the lease this late payment will be assessed a fee of $_____.

Should the rent not be paid over a period of one month we have the option to instruct our attorneys to initiate a legal eviction proceeding. To keep your account current and avoid litigation, please submit your full rent plus the additional fee today.

Sincerely,

Landlord

BILL TO TENANT FOR DAMAGES

Date: _____

To: _____

It has been necessary to repair damage to the premises that you occupy. According to our Rental Agreement the tenant is responsible for the cost of repairing damages to the rental premises that were done by the tenant or the tenant's invitees. The cost of the repairs were as follows: (Receipts are attached)

_____

_____

_____

_____

_____

_____

_____   _____ - _____
LANDLORD   PHONE

LETTER OF NON-RENEWAL OF LEASE

Date: _____

Dear _____,

This letter is to remind you that your lease will expire on _____. Please be advised that we do not intend to renew or extend your lease for the rental premises

The keys should be delivered to the address below on or before the end of the lease along with your forwarding address. Within thirty (30) days of the lease termination, we will inspect the premises for damages, deduct any amounts necessary for repairs, and refund the balance of your security deposit.

Should you not vacate the premises at the end of the lease, please be aware of the financial and legal penalties that are enumerated in your lease. If you have any questions, please call.

Sincerely,

Landlord
(Address, phone number)

MOVE-OUT LETTER

Date: _____

Dear _____,

Your scheduled move out date is _____. Please contact our office so we can schedule the freight elevator for your move. We have several sizes of moving boxes available for our tenants in the office.

Within thirty days after you move out, we will inspect your unit for damage in order to calculate your return on the security deposit. If you wish to save a cleaning charge, we do have cleaning supplies that our staff uses to prepare units.

Please remember to drop off the keys to your unit and to any storage facilities at the office. We also ask that you provide us with a forwarding address where we can send your portion of the security deposit.

If you need any assistance, please call the office.

Sincerely,

Landlord

SECURITY DEPOSIT ITEMIZATION

RENTAL PREMISES: _____

RENTED TO: _____

DATE INSPECTED: _____

SECURITY DEPOSIT: $_____

ITEM: REPAIR/CLEANING/ REPLACE	ESTIMATE	PARTS	LABOR	TOTAL

AMOUNT OF SECURITY DEPOSIT RETURNED $_____

{Attach copies of estimates, receipts, and bills.}

About the Author

Diana Brodman Summers received her JD from DePaul University College of Law and her undergraduate degree from Roosevelt University. She is an arbitrator for both the Cook and DuPage County mandatory arbitration programs. Ms. Summers is an active member of the DuPage County Bar Association, National Employment Lawyers Association, the American Bar Association, and the Illinois State Bar Association.

Ms. Summers has taught seminars for lawyers through several bar associations and has written articles on computerizing law offices. She currently maintains a law practice in Lisle, Illinois, a suburb of Chicago.